Especially for you from
Washington Speakers Bureau

CUSTOMER LOVE

ATTRACTING AND KEEPING CUSTOMERS FOR LIFE

CHIP R. BELL

For permissions requests, contact the publisher at:

    Executive Excellence Publishing
    1344 East 1120 South
    Provo, UT 84606
    phone: 1-801-375-4060
    toll free: 1-800-304-9782
    fax: 1-801-377-5960
    www.eep.com

For Executive Excellence books, magazines and other products, contact Executive Excellence directly. Call 1-800-304-9782, fax 1-801-377-5960, or visit our Web site at www.eep.com.

Printed in the United States

10 9 8 7 6 5 4 3 2 1

Cover design by Nichole Klein

Printed by Publishers Press

Library of Congress Cataloging-in-Publication Data

ISBN: 1-890009-78-4

Dedicated to Ron Zemke

ACKNOWLEDGMENTS

Composing this acknowledgment page reminds me of all the many people in my life who have taught me valuable lessons in love. Most people get their first lessons in love from their immedieate family. I am grateful to my parents, Avis and Ray, my brother Jack and my sister Christa. Other lessons came from important teachers, coaches, professors, friends, and kinfolk—too numerous to name.

Adult lessons came from my partners, Ron Zemke and Tom Connellan, as well as close colleagues Oren Harari, Glenn Kiser, Bruce Fritch, Larry Davis, Patsy Jane and Larry Hollar, Lisa Williams Bell, Tony Lay, Karen and Jimmie Steele, Jill Applegate, Karen Revill, Heather Shea, Tammy Richards, Cliff and Debbie Dickinson, and the wonderful folks at the Washington Speakers Bureau. I am also grateful to the many clients over the last 25 years who have taught me enormous lessons in customer love.

This book had its own special cast of love influencers. Leslie Stephen, my world-class editor and long-term friend, was there as always with her special brand of vernacular wisdom. Steve Piersanti, at Berrett-Koehler Publishing, provided early advocacy and perpetual devotion. The capable staff, at Executive Excellence Publishing, supportively managed the book production process. And clearly this book would not have happened without the vision and encouragement of Ken Shelton, editor-in-chief of Executive Excellence Publishing.

Finally, my *graduate* education in love came from my immediate family: my son Bilijack, my daughter-in-law Lisa, and my wife Nancy. Their unconditional love, tireless support, and enthusiastic devotion is the very essence of what this book strives to be about.

To all of you, my heartfelt thanks.

TABLE OF CONTENTS

PART C: THE PRACTICE

PREFACE

Why write the "Book of Love?" The impetus for this book came from several directions. The renaissance of customer service has raised the bar to such a point that organizations are ready to consider "love" as a behavioral expression of customer devotion. After all, customer don't generally say, "I like dealing with _____ (fill in the blank with your favorite service provider)"; they use the "L" word. When organizations like Southwest Airlines use *LUV* as their stock symbol, when formerly stiff-upper-lip senior executives unabashedly embrace front-line employees at awards ceremonies, when hard-nosed CEOs like GE's Jack Welch or Harley-Davidson's Rich Teerlink or America OnLine's Steve Case speak of passion and deep values in the same breath as "bottom line," it signals an era of accepting old-fashioned, lump-in-your-throat concepts.

Another impetus for writing this book came from a senior manager at Marriott. Bridget Bilinsky, now VP for Franchising at Courtyard by Marriott, said, "When I was general manager of a property, I wanted my customers to 'fall in love' with our hotel." I had never thought of a romantic crush as a goal for customer service. Ken Blanchard was onto a sports version of that end when he wrote of "raving fans." Carl Sewell took the forever-and-ever angle when he wrote of "customers for life." Len Berry took the research side of heart-felt service when he wrote of the "soul of service."

After *Customers As Partners* was published in 1994, many people sent me notes, commenting that the depth of customer allegiance was not singularly anchored to length of relationship. The word "partnership" generally implies a relationship that is deeper and longer than normal. They convinced me that some transactions of short duration could possess a "love at first sight" quality that equalled the depth of a solid partnership. I realized I had more to say about customer relationships.

I also realized that, as customers, we can be *wowed*, yet still not be *wooed*. Walt Disney World *wows* me; I am delighted and as giddy as a kid on her first trip to the zoo. But my emotions are the superficial, fleeting sensations that come from watching a stirring movie or an exciting ballgame. Ritz-Carlton Hotels, on the other hand, *woos* me; I am so moved and enchanted by such a refined experience that the memory and the feeling stay with me long past checkout. Now, my Ritz-Carlton might be your DisneyWorld, but the difference between the two is clear. What happens to us that turns allure into allegiance? What is the anatomy of customer love? And, what can organizations do to attract customer love?

Customer love is more than a serendipitous, starry-eyed moment when everything happens right and the customer is infatuated, although we can "love" a service provider that we encounter only once or infrequently. "Love" is code for many emotions: adoration, devotion, and passionate attachment. It is that warm feeling you get when you feel a special, sometimes unexplainable connection. It is a sense of positive longing and pleasant nostalgia, when your memory of that last experience bubbles to the surface of your brain. When you "smile to yourself" if the service provider's name is mentioned, you are "in love." This book is about inspiring those feelings.

This book is not about playing customer cupid, though. There is clearly a simple philosophy on which this book is grounded, but it is not a quiver of special arrows to ensnare the emotion of the customer. Tricks are the tools of service

Casanova's who see customer love all as a ploy of seduction, and thus a game to be won. True customer service is never about winning and losing. It is not about clever conquest. It is a special and consecrated invitation to exchange gifts.

This book is also not research-based. As valuable as research can be, love is a poor subject for the autopsy of objectivity. We can predict retention; we cannot predict infatuation. We can predict that loyalty might occur. We cannot accurately predict the point when appeal and temporary fervor are converted to an unshakable commitment. This book follows the outlook captured in a quote from John Steinbeck's *Sea of Cortez*:

> The Mexican sierra fish has 17 plus 15 plus nine spines in the dorsal fin. These can easily be counted. But if the sierra strikes hard on the line so that your hands are burned, if the fish sounds and nearly escapes and finally comes in over the rail, his colors pulsing and his tail beating in the air, a whole new relational externality has come into being—an entity which is more than the sum of the fish plus the fisherman.

This book is about the enchantment of service—more along the lines of "if you build it, they will come." A wise person once told me, "Trust love. Even if your love of a person is in deep water, stay in love with love. Your trust in love will bring you to the other side." I think that trust is equally plausible when the target of our love is a customer. If we approach the relationship from the position of love, we will rarely be forsaken and often be richly rewarded with the joy of service, and sometimes with the loyalty of the customer.

Woven throughout this book is a belief that attracting customer love requires a special organizational culture. Customers see the organization through the attitude and practices of the people they encounter. Customer confidence in a organization's capacity and desire to back its front-line ambassador is either confirmed or dashed by what that ambassador says and does.

While there are diligent souls who give great service despite the inadequacies of the organization they front, sooner or later the customer sees what is behind the front guard. And if that scene fails to match their expectations, confidence is eroded and the shine quickly wears off the relationship.

Some of the concepts in this book have appeared in other books I have written, although I have updated them a bit. Some of what we know about serving customers has not changed since Sears was Sears Roebuck and Co. and their competition was Montgomery Ward, not Wal-Mart. But other things have changed. The path to attracting customer love today is a rockier one than in days past. Customers are less patient, more finicky, less trusting, and more astute regarding the worth of service than before. Efforts to attract and nurture them must take into account their new attitudes and standards.

Introduction: How to Get the Most from This Book

Knowing what to expect is a good start to getting the most from this book. This book is simply organized into three parts, focusing on the why, what, and how. Actually, all three queries are woven into all the chapters. But the choice and placement of chapters in the book generally follows the why-what-how organization.

Part I: The Picture

Chapter 1: What's Love Got to Do with It (Business)? Plenty. It's the *alpha* and *omega* of every successful business. Also included in this chapter is a case study on customer love in action—Leroy Clark lived the philosophy this book is about.

Chapter 2: The "Just for Today" Anatomy of Customer Love. Anatomies are models; they show us how all the parts *should* be. This chapter provides the model upon which the book is constructed. In so doing, it begins to speak for the rationale of customer love. "Just for Today" is a not-so-subtle reminder that, when it comes to customer loyalty, what works today might not be so compelling tomorrow.

Chapter 3: Customer Love Unwrapped. At one point, I considered calling this chapter "The 'Just for Today' Anatomy of Customer Love Part Two" because it illustrates the model in story form. Just as Leroy reflects the attitude, Mrs. Ashley demonstrates the approach.

PART II: THE PARTS

Chapter 4: Inclusion: Customers Will Care When They Share. This is the first stop on the way to customer love. It makes the case that customers today expect to involved in unique and unusual ways. If the customers of yesteryear desired more of a master-slave relationship ("the customer is king"), customers today (most of them) want more of a partnership. And to partner, you have to have some skin in the game.

Chapter 5: Connection: The Magic Touch of Service. Partners are not without a connection—that tie that binds in a fashion that reminds us both of our interdependence as well as our humanity. "Touch" has many meanings beyond physical contact. Think of the connotation of "being touched" by a great movie, a poignant sermon, or a spectacular sunset. This chapter explores how the service encounter is something very special when devotion is the goal.

Chapter 6: Enlightenment: Growing Customer Love. If lack of communication is the primary cause of divorce, lack of growth has to be a close second. Always a key part of valued relationships, growth is now a part of the customer-service provider prescription for loyalty. As customers struggle to keep current and up-to-date, they value service providers who work hard, not only to stay in a constant state of learning but also to support the growth of their customers.

Chapter 7: Trust: Affirming a Covenant with Customers. Ask 20 people the most important attribute of great relationships, and 19 will mention "trust." Trust is an emotional blend of reliability, assurance, and certainty. It is the principal building block of confidence. Service providers in pursuit of customer devotion will only get as far as the customer's confidence goes.

Chapter 8: Betrayal: Dealing with Our Own Guilt. Long-term customer relationships without a screw-up are as rare as hen's teeth. Even though wise service providers work hard to prevent error, they work even harder to recover effectively when service fails and the customer is disappointed. Service recovery is a double-sided coin—internal and external. This chapter deals with how we effectively deal with our guilt when we let down a valued customer.

Chapter 9: Betrayal: Dealing with a Lover's Scorn. Service recovery is more than damage control. It is also far more than problem resolution. Fundamentally, effective service recovery means healing a broken relationship. Customers who have a problem and witness the service provider dealing with the breakdown end up being more loyal than customers who have never had a problem. This chapter outlines powerful techniques for effectively dealing with disappointed customers.

Chapter 10: Empowerment: Keeping Customers in Control. The new anatomy of customer devotion puts the customer in control. This arrangement comes in part from the realization that customers are living in the midst of massive change. Many cope to keep up; some struggle to stay on top. When they find a service provider that helps them be and feel more powerful, their loyalty soars. The source of customer power comes from dealing with an organization of service people who exhibit the confidence and competence of high performers on their game. This chapter outlines the route to creating an empowered customer through an empowered front line.

Chapter 11: Enchantment: The Magic of the Occasional Miracle. We have all experienced or heard about those service moments when someone pulled out all the stops. Whether recipient or witness, such unexpected, out-of-the-box encounters remind us that service miracles can still happen. Such special incidents leave us as enthralled as candlelight and champagne on a special date. This chapter outlines when and how enchantment can help nurture customer affection.

Chapter 12: Elasticity: Putting Stretch in the Relationship. Great relationships are not 50-50. That idea provokes a win-lose, score-keeping mentality. Healthy partnerships are built on the principle of floating reciprocity—the idea that elasticity is more valued than tolerance, and adaptability more important than patience. This chapter reframes what *fairness* means and offers ways to be a willow, not an oak, in the winds of customer demands.

Chapter 13: Generosity: Giving More than You Expect to Get. Customers remain loyal to service providers who act more interested in maximizing the value of the relationship than minimizing the transaction cost. Great relationships are giving relationships. They harbor an abundance mentality, seeking ways to give without perpetual preoccupation with return.

PART III: THE PRACTICE

Chapter 14: The Leader of a Customer Love Culture. In today's world, cultures are built and sustained through the actions of leaders. While we are gradually shedding the concept of leader as surrogate parent and evolving a concept of leadership that focuses on followership, what leaders do counts toward what gets attention. This chapter provides a context for examining the many functions of the leader in a customer-love culture.

Chapter 15: The Love Leader as Listener. Leaders of customer love are dramatic listeners. Poor communication is not only the most frequent predictor of divorce in marriage, but it holds true for organizational success as well. Leaders in a customer-love culture listen dramatically (so there is no doubt they are listening), demonstrate lavish understanding, and respond in ways that indicate customer input is valued and makes a difference.

Chapter 16: The Love Leader as Trust Giver. A customer-love culture can only happen within a climate of trust. Leaders who give trust start with self-esteem healthy enough to take emotional risks with associates and customers. They replace control with support, and substitute acceptance for guilt. They know that only through an atmosphere of trust will employees perpetually act with integrity and confidence.

Chapter 17: The Love Leader as Empowerer. Empowerment does not mean unlimited license. It means responsible freedom.

The leaders in a customer-love culture treat empowerment as a process of eliminating barriers, of freeing employees to use their personal power to meet customer needs and solve customer challenges. This chapter examines the most common barriers to empowered actions and suggests practical leadership actions.

Chapter 18: The Love Leader as Mentor. The new definition of customer devotion includes a requirement for growth. Customers like dealing with organizations that help them learn; they feel confident dealing with an organization that is itself constantly learning, improving, and evolving. To be seen by the customer as a learning organization suggests that leaders are mentors, helping their employees stay in a constant state of learning. This chapter offers both a philosophical perspective and a pragmatic primer on how leaders act as mentors to the people they manage and lead.

Chapter 19: The Love Leader as Passion Bearer. Customers *like* dealing with employees who demonstrate commitment; they *love* dealing with employees who demonstrate passion. Passion is a tag for that infectious energy that reflects a zeal to be the best, a deep dedication to one's role, and an obvious show of pride. Customers not only derive confidence from such interpersonal connections, they fuel their own sense of well-being. Leaders must be passion bearers, modeling the excitement they want employees to transmit to customers.

Chapter 20: The Love Leader a Change Agent. Change is a crucial requirement for organizations wishing to survive and thrive in today's economy. If you aren't "making dust," you are "eating dust." Appropriate change directed toward the customer experience mitigates against boredom and sameness. It implies an organization that is evergreen in its attitude and its offerings. Tom Peters said, "We are all in the fashion business." Those organizations unwilling to make their own products and services obsolete will be made obsolete by their competitors. It means having leaders who are agents or allies of change —who embrace it, understand it, welcome it, and maximize the opportunities presented by it. This chapter provides a new look at change, why resistance sometimes occurs, and how to function effectively as an ambassador of change.

Chapter 21: Reinventing Service with Love in Mind. The practical side of effective change management is the capacity to reinvent service. This unique chapter provides several innovation tools leaders can use to rebuild or reinvigorate their service to customers. The key to reinventing service is to recognize that, as the core of product is physical form, the core of service is emotional feeling.

Chapter 22: Homestyle Customer Love. This chapter is aimed at providing a sense of what it looks like and sounds like when a culture is operating as a customer-love environment. Built around an actual experience at a major hotel, this chapter is the group version of customer love in action.

Chapter 23: How the Customer Gets Love. We are all customers. Sometimes the examination of customer love from the perspective of "how to get service providers to love the customer" can offer helpful insights. In part, this chapter is about how to get great service. It is also about an attitude imperative for a love relationship. Healthy love relationships have an expectancy of greatness, an energy focused on making things work, an openness about needs and goals, a bountiful display of respect, and a quickness to express gratitude and generosity.

Chapter 24: Affirming Customer Love. The old adage, "What gets rewarded gets repeated" is a powerful reminder that if we want our associates to deliver customer love . . . and, if we are anxious for our customers to return love, we must find ways to affirm actions associated with customer loyalty. This chapter provides a unique look at how to maximize affirmation by directing our energy at a target other than the associate or customer.

Chapter 25: 25 Ways to Show Customer Love. This final chapter makes the point that customer devotion cannot be sustained if it is taken for granted. It must receive ceaseless care and attention. I offer 25 techniques for expressing that attention as a seed list to start affection growing.

Scan this book, read it from front to back, or back to front. How you read it is not important. What matters is that you *do something* with what you gain. Make a pledge to start the love connection with your next customer. Ignore the past, raise your hopes to greater planes, and make it happen. You know that passion is infectious. People smile at you, and what do you do? You smile back. A stranger waves at you, and you acknowledge his or her greeting. *Passion* (Pass-I-on) is a way of getting revenge against a challenging, difficult, and often indifferent world. So go infect someone with your service passion. Fall in love with "customer love" and watch what happens.

Don't save this book. This is not a reference book. You are not likely to go back and pull it off the shelf to check a formula, quote, or reference. So, give the darn thing away. Select a soul who most needs to "fall in love" with a customer and give this book to him or her. No fanfare, no cute or caustic note, just simply say, "I liked this book and thought you might enjoy reading it."

Finally, let me know what you think. This is the shortest book I have ever written, and I hope it makes a difference. My goal was to create a book that people would "fall in love with" to start something with their customers. The "About the Author" page contains all the information you need to contact me. I do invite your feedback. Who knows? I might decide to write another little book like this.

Chip R. Bell
Dallas, Texas

1

WHAT'S LOVE GOT TO DO WITH IT (BUSINESS)?

Customer service has been on a roller coaster ride for the last 15 years. In the mid-80s, the buzzword was "customer satisfaction." Winners worked hard to understand and meet customer needs. Satisfaction was the brass ring of choice and the corporate drumbeat began its roll. Banners, bands, and banter told employees to start focusing on satisfying the customer. After all, the customer was always right.

In the 90s, the customer service bar got raised. As quality initiatives started impacting product quality, simply *satisfying* the customer was viewed as nothing more than the price of admission in the game to *win* the customer. The real winners focused on customer retention. While the first wave of the 80s was punctuated by stories of Disney, Nordstrom, Stew Leonard's Dairy, and words like "wowing," "outrageous," and "raving fans," this new emphasis on retention came replete with graphs and numbers, which keyed off of the lifetime worth of a customer. The motto became, "Keep the customer for life, and your bottom line will be the envy of the industry." Names like Sewell, Reichheld, and Sasser were the key prophets in the customer-retention revival.

Toward the end of the 1990s, customer retention got a new wrinkle—personalized service. The development of data-mining technology enabled organizations to gain and retain large amounts of information about the customer . . . not just demographics and financial information, but buying preferences and behavior. This enabled organizations to focus on customized (or as one popular business evangelist put it, "customerized") service. "One" became the key number—as in one-to-one (a la Peppers & Rogers, Pine & Gilmore) and one size fits one (a la Heil, et al). Amazon.com and Ritz-Carlton became the exemplars. Organizations acquired tools and software to capture more information about the customer than you'd find in a crackerjack salesperson's "little black book." The thesis was this: Make customers perceive they are your only customer, and you'll win their loyalty.

Customers benefitted greatly from all three initiatives: satisfaction, retention and customization. These initiatives have raised service quality. While customers still get lousy service more often than they would like, most would agree that service quality is better overall than it was 15 years ago. This is partly because customer expectations for service have gone up, often to the chagrin of service superstars, who now have new customers walk in and think, "Okay, I've heard about you people— now blow my mind." The path to pleasing customers has led to efforts to make work life more positive for employees, as organizations have learned how much employee relations impact customer relations. As organizations have organized better for service delivery, the cost of providing good service has gone down. As organizations have learned about the power of alliances and partnerships, access to resources has increased.

THE NEXT WAVE

So where is customer service going in the future? Toward love! The big kahuna of customer loyalty is devotion—in a word, love. Organizations that manage to attract and nurture a customer's love win big. And what do they win?

Customers who *like* you will come back. But customers who *love* you will go out of their way to take care of you. They don't just come back, they don't simply recommend you, they *insist* their friends do business with you. They forgive you when you make mistakes and defend you to others who have bad experiences with you. They give you candid feedback when they spot (or experience) a problem, even if you sometimes take their feedback for granted. They never sue or threaten to sue. In fact, it would never occur to them to sue.

Loving customers become your best sales force, championing you to others. Because they know you (and your processes), they can be less expensive to service. And because they feel committed to you and see value in emotional and experiential terms, they will pay more for what they get from you—because they are convinced it is worth it. They can be more demanding than the customer who is simply satisfied. But their enormous impact on your bottom line as well as your marketplace presence make them more than worth the extra maintenance they may require.

University of Texas professor Robert Peterson's research indicates that when customers use the "L" word (or other emotion-laden terms of endearment) to describe you, their buying habits are dramatically different from those who simply like you. In fact, he found that 85 percent of the customers who claimed "satisfaction" would leave you for a competitor. The pursuit of customer love is not about personalization, although that can certainly be a component.

The quest for customer love is not about the economics of lifetime value, although customers who love you are more likely to stay with you over time. The "love" strategy is the one the merchant in your hometown uses when he treats you as a neighbor, not a consumer. It is not a complex strategy, although it can be difficult to implement, particularly in an organization with many customers and service providers.

There is a Native American ceremony called the "sweat lodge," the goal of which is spiritual cleansing. When it works, participants claim they are visited by a deity in some form, such as an eagle, wolf, or deer. While the pinnacle is the surprise visit, much work goes into getting ready. And the process is as important as the outcome. A hut is built. Rocks are chosen, heated red hot, and then placed in a hole in the center of the floor of the hut. As naked (or nearly naked) participants sweat, pray, sweat, chant, sweat, smoke the peace pipe (did I say sweat?), their ritual creates the stage for the appearance of the deity, who often speaks through a participant or medicine man.

If the stage is improperly set—if the participants are not emotionally ready—there is no appearance. At times, participants do everything correctly, but the deity never visits. It is a gentle reminder that visits are not the result of a formula, but the byproduct of faith. With disappointment, they dismiss to repeat the sweat lodge ritual another day.

Customer love is like a sweat lodge. You can do your best to create a stage for love and still come up short. Customer love, like all other forms of love, is a serendipitous event, far more about magic than method.

CUSTOMER LOVE IN ACTION

Leroy Clark was the grocer in my South Georgia hometown, my introduction to what it meant to be a "merchant"—courteous and eager to help all who came into his small, all-purpose store. His style bore no resemblance to the style of Shakespeare's Venice-based merchant, the one debated hotly in Mrs. Wilcox's sophomore English class—Mr. Clark would never think of demanding a "pound of flesh," even from the most ruthless customer.

Today, the corporate world is rediscovering the sense of service that permeated Leroy Clark's bones. This "rediscovery" is made to sound like a major breakthrough—something absent from the past, newly found, and terribly important. Every business journal seems to trumpet superior customer service almost like *Life* magazine's coverage of the 1969 walk on the moon. The Leroy Clarks of yesteryear get no credit for using methods now attributed to Disney, Ritz-Carlton Hotels, Federal Express, Nordstrom, and the like.

What happened between the early 1950s version of small-town service and the present-day renaissance of that same orientation? How did the business world move so far away from Leroy Clark, and why is his brand of customer service now so eagerly sought? Can it be that Leroy could teach us lessons about personal service relevant for the new millennium?

Before you chide me that superior service involves much more than neighborly manners, let me quickly add that Leroy Clark knew a lot about a service vision, customer-friendly delivery systems, service recovery, and front-line empowerment. To be sure, Leroy was no scholar of service management, nor a graduate of customer-relations training classes. He did what he did out of a solid grounding in the premise that serving implied a devotion to the customer. Service, to Leroy, was about reciprocal power—his power to provide goods and services coupled with the customer's power to keep him in business.

He was clear on his role: to provide groceries and a few small appliances to a small, rural community. He didn't get hung up on "being the best" or "improving the bottom line." He gave no thought to franchising, diversifying, merging, or acquiring. He simply provided groceries to his neighbors at a fair price. He did not have to remind himself to "stick to his knitting" or "stay close to his customers." He had few pretensions, no aspirations to rise to baronial or congressional status, and meager managerial tools to lead him astray. Leroy was a merchant, and that was that. He possessed a responsibility to those who crossed the threshold of his grocery store.

Leroy acted out of a simple belief: "My customers are my neighbors." To cheat, disappoint, or dissatisfy a customer would be as inappropriate as starting a heated argument at a family reunion. And he would no more question the honesty of a customer than he would accuse one of his two daughters of stealing. He believed his customers were honest—and they always seemed to be. He also assumed that differences with customers would be resolved with a sense of fair play—and they always seemed to be.

Leroy knew what his customers needed and expected. One day, my father, a full-time banker and full-time farmer, stopped in to buy a loaf of bread. "Mr. Bell," said Leroy, in his always polite voice, "I ordered you some of those fly strips for your pig house. Last time you were in here, you mentioned that the flies were about to take away your new farrowing house." I wonder how many service organizations would stock an item based solely on data gathered through eavesdropping or "fair weather" conversation. Leroy cared a lot more about service than inventory. And when my father opted to *not* buy the sticky, yellow fly strips, Leroy acted neither hurt nor disappointed. He knew his role and responsibility—and he fulfilled both.

Leroy rearranged his grocery store every year or so. "Customers are forever telling me better ways to set up the store," he said one midsummer day, when I was in town to buy a lawn mower blade at Hinson's Hardware and stopped by the New City Market to also buy a Forever Yours candy bar and an RC cola. "I'm not always real crazy about their ideas," he admitted, "but if I didn't make a few changes, they'd think I didn't have any respect for them." And if there was a new fad, Leroy would have it in stock in a hurry. He had Hula Hoops and Fire Balls before the big stores in Macon had them!

Today we marvel at the superstar companies—3M, USAA, Southwest Airlines, Amazon.com—that make a fetish of listening and responding to customers. Leroy knew how to listen; he also knew how to convince his customers that their input was valued and respected. Oh, I realize it's much easier with one store and a stable customer base. But I'll bet Leroy would have figured out how to listen dramatically if he'd been the president of The Great Atlantic and Pacific Tea Company. It was in his nature to pay attention to those he served.

Though I dare say he never used the word in his whole life, Leroy was a master at creating an atmosphere of *love*—especially with his only stock boy. Working hard one day to open a case of butter beans, the young man was embarrassed by a cruel, racial slur thrown at him by a couple of loud, white teenagers. "You don't have the brains of a ..," they rudely jeered. Leroy calmly walked over to the rowdy boys and sternly demanded that they leave. Before they were out of earshot, he turned to the stock boy and said, "Adel, I'm going to the bank. You know what to do, so you're in charge of the store while I'm gone."

Now, that's small potatoes in today's high-rise, corporate world. But in a very conservative, racially biased small Georgia country town in the early 1950s, it was empowerment with a capital 'E'. I'm not saying Leroy was a saint without prejudice. But Leroy knew that the stock boy would probably get more "Can you help me find?" questions than he would. And he knew that if this young man was treated with respect and importance, he would more likely exhibit confidence and competence when serving a patron of the store. What would Leroy think today if he knew his leadership practices were the goal of senior executives who are paid more in a year than Leroy earned in a lifetime?

Leroy was also effective at recovering from a customer-service breakdown. There was no need for a written, published "service guarantee"—Leroy *was* the guarantee. He would not even consider offering a discount if something customers purchased was not up to their expectations. Instead of some version of "$3 off if it's late," "You don't owe me a thing" was his invariable response. We need more Leroys instead of merchants who too frequently argue over an 89-cent item with a customer who, if loyal to that same store, could spend $40,000 over the average eight years of living in a given location.

Leroy also knew that if any of his customers had a problem, his initial focus had to be on fixing the relationship with that customer. Only then could he deal with the customer's problem. For example, my grandmother once bought an ice cream churn from Leroy—the kind grandsons endlessly hand crank to turn cold, thick cream into a summer eve's delight. It was a hot July day when she first unpacked it, only to discover the crank was missing. "Leroy," she complained over the phone, "you sold me a bum steer!" Well, Leroy drove three miles out in the country with another churn. With him, he brought a fresh-baked apple pie and two gallons of "store bought" ice cream. Now, here is the best part: He sat out in the shade for half an hour with my grandmother, quizzing her on her secrets for getting azaleas to grow big and healthy.

I suppose I'm on thin ice by implying that it's possible to simplify a very challenging issue. A few of the many complex barriers to replicating Leroy's brand of customer love include corporate bigness, bureaucracy, legal restrictions, diverse customer requirements, increased competition domestically and internationally, and scarcity of committed and competent service employees. And if it was as easy now as it was years ago in South Georgia, great service books would not become bestsellers, nor would corporations hire service consultants to help them figure out ways to ensure customers' loyalty.

Yet, sometimes I wonder if the question of customer loyalty is much simpler than we realize. Perhaps we just need to rekindle and nurture the passion to give customers the kind of love that guided Leroy Clark. It's possible that I am just a romantic, opting for nostalgia instead of accepting the cold reality of the present. But then again, maybe not.

2

THE "JUST FOR TODAY" ANATOMY OF CUSTOMER LOVE

Love (luv), n. v., 1. a feeling of warm personal attachment or deep affection. 2. strong predilection or liking for anything. 3. to have a profoundly passionate affection for. 4. to have a steadfast, enduring loyalty toward. 5. to adore.

Love is the subject of more songs and books than any single topic. But you won't find the topic represented in the business section of your library, favorite book store, or Web site. Wonder why? We certainly are not timid about using the word *love* when describing a great service experience. We talk about the people who deliver world-class service with the same affectionate tones we use to speak of family and close friends.

When we think of bad service—or, more specifically, our typical service experiences—we might consider "customer love" to be an extreme oxymoron, like *civil war*, *jumbo shrimp*, or *married life* (just kidding). While "plain vanilla" may describe today's typical service, most customers have "fallen in love" with some service provider somewhere along the way. Since those moments happen rarely, customers begin to long for them. They also "cruise" the marketplace in search of those able to make love happen.

My dad was a big fan of the *Mutt and Jeff* comic strip. When I was a little boy, I remember him reading it as religiously as he listened to *The Shadow* and *Johnny Dollar* on our radio. One of his favorite strips portrayed Mutt saying to Jeff, "If everybody saw like I did, everybody would want my wife." To which Jeff responded, "If everybody saw like I did, *nobody* would want your wife." It was my early introduction to the "eye of the beholder" idea.

Customer love is as complex as any other type of love. Love is a highly personalized experience. Like Mutt and Jeff, what attracts me to a service provider might be completely different from what attracts you. For instance, I have a friend whose idea of the perfect hotel check-in is to be able to get from the curb out front into the room in less than 30 seconds, without eye contact or conversation with a living soul. For me, that seems completely unnatural. Unless it is very late or I am confronted with a long wait, I would rather chat with the front desk clerk, build a personal bond I might need later, influence the choice of room I get, and make someone smile. My friend also likes single malt scotch, red corvettes, and ice fishing—it takes all kinds!

The anatomy of customer love is like a dart board. Touching any part of the anatomy will yield us some points, like when the dart hits the target somewhere. But the value of each area is unique to each of us. My 50-point bullseye might be something quite different from your bullseye.

Attracting customer love begins with understanding customers well enough to get a fine bead on their target. It requires dramatic listening and lavish understanding. It means remembering that the "turn-on" of today might not be the same in the future. As organizations rush to install the technological capacity to store and respond to customer preferences, they erroneously assume that preferences are static and forever. For instance, if my travel agent assumed my preference for an aisle seat was engraved in stone, she would disappoint me when my Dallas-to-Los Angeles flight took me over the Grand Canyon at sunset and I was unable to enjoy the splendor of that rare view.

That said, what are the components that attract most customers most of the time? The model below shows the pieces that will be explored in depth in chapters to come. As we explore them, remember that all of them are not required to maximize attraction. And the value of any particular part is dependent on the customer. Remember *Mutt and Jeff*!

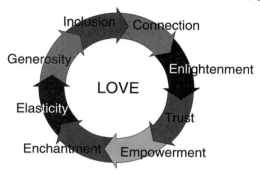

INCLUDE ME

"Dinner on the ground" was code for participation when I was growing up. While the event went with all family reunions, this special form of community most often occurred after certain church services. The church version followed four congregational hymns, a few announcements, a choir special, 35 minutes of hard (and loud) preaching, ending with a guilt-rendering call to the altar while the choir hummed one more verse of "Just as I Am." If you were a fidgety kid, it was the longest hour of your life.

"Dinner on the ground" was a super event for little boys; we could run, holler, and pull ponytails pretty much unsupervised, since our caretakers were occupied with set-up and clean-up. For the women, it was a time to show off a new recipe or the fact that you had grown the biggest squash in the county (my mother usually won that contest.) Over sweet ice tea men told tales of the one that got away or compared their prowess with baseball trivia. The minister frowned a lot, until he had said the blessing. You went home after eating way too much fried chicken and deep-dish peach pie. But this "everyone bring something" event brought people closer and enabled them to feel more interdependent. It was *community* in its purest form. And

31

it was a sad day for this love feast when someone got the bright idea of "just calling Big Al and having him bring the barbecue with all the trimmings."

Good feelings about a service provider can increase dramatically when customers have a chance to "put some skin in the game." Inclusion not only captures the creativity and competence of customers as they serve with you, but their commitment and allegiance rise as well. The secret is knowing when and how to include, because sometimes customers are not interested in participation. And many times the inclusion of customers is inappropriate. Wise service providers attract customer love by making the "dinner on the ground" side of service as fun, memorable, and wholesome as a church picnic.

CONNECT WITH ME

One of this century's biggest movie hits was Steven Spielberg's *ET: The Extraterrestrial*. The heart-warming film used as its billboard symbol the outstretched, magical finger of the extraterrestrial main character. The pose carried a spiritual symbolism not unlike Michaelangelo's masterpiece in the Sistine Chapel.

Every religion has relied on the power of touch. Likewise, every civilized society has used some form of touch as the gesture of social intimacy. Touch litters our language. "Let's shake on it" is a token of agreement. "Give her a hand" is an invitation for affirmation. Giving one's "hand in marriage" communicates a symbol of union. "Touch" is itself a loaded word. Its meanings range from physical contact (as in, "Don't touch that hot stove.") to emotional connection (as in, "That book really touched me.") to style (as in, "He has that special touch."). All of these meanings are relevant for attracting customer love.

Service is more than a process by which we get our needs met. It is an experience that resonates with our heart, a rendezvous that engages our emotions. The manner in which the service provider manages these experiences can turn a routine encounter into a magical moment. The emotional touch of service is the connection that can kindle a sense of kinship and stimulate a bond of loyalty.

TEACH ME

"In times of massive change," wrote philosopher Eric Hoffer, "it is the learner who will inherit the earth, while the learned stay elegantly tied to a world that no longer exists." Customers have learned that their thrivability is anchored in their capacity to keep up. They expect service providers to educate them.

There are customers who enjoy learning for learning's sake. They are the ones who stayed after class in college to ask the professor another question. When there was an "extra points" question on the final exam, they always answered it—most of us were lucky to have time to answer the regular questions. These are the customers who read the manual . . . first!

Most customers learn for a purpose—one obvious and relevant to them at the moment. Most customers want the service education process to be hassle-free. They want it subtle or fun or rewarding. In fact, the learning experience with the greatest attraction is one in which the attraction is embedded in the experience. Not that it has to be subliminal or obtuse—it can be right out front. But, it needs to seem like a part of the service experience, not an add-on or extra part.

SHOW ME THE TRUST

Research indicates that reliability is the attribute customers view as most important. But there is a level above reliability, and it is the stuff trust is made of. Reliability is what we do to convince the customer that *we* can be trusted. But covenants are brokered on two-way trust. Customer love begins with actions that tell customers *they* are trusted. It is the leap of faith that service providers take that involves some level of risk.

Love starts with trust, and as strange as it may sound, love is solidified through betrayal. Customers are gun shy of service providers until they witness service recovery. Before service failure, there is only hope; after service failure, there is proof. It is through the effective management of betrayal that customers truly come to trust. Think about it. Recall all the great service stories you have heard in your life. Most are about heroics when things go wrong.

This does not imply that service providers should intentionally screw up so they can fix it well. It does mean that we should take enough risk to create a likely potential for a mistake, and then handle the service betrayal with the care of a great friend. Restoration heroics take a culture in which service people view mistakes as a chance to learn and customer complaints as valuable gifts.

HELP ME BE STRONG

Empowerment is a term historically reserved for employees, slaves, and submissive spouses. The focus has been on helping the powerful share power with the powerless. Empowerment has been sold as the boon to creativity, productivity, and high morale. It is rarely used in the context of customer service. Yet, customers desire power and control in their lives. They are attracted to service providers that are intent on helping them gain that power.

Empowerment is not a gift bestowed; it is a force released. Customer power surfaces when the service experience reminds customers of their capacity, their influence, and their allies. Power is about strength and control, not command or might. It is an energy to be channeled usefully, not a shield to exclude and oppress.

My fifth grade teacher was Mrs. Pope. She paddled more kids than all the other teachers combined. She took her teaching as seriously as she did her disciplining. One day, she announced that Mr. Lancaster, the principal of the school, had asked her to select a student to go with him to a nearby town and bring back a large trophy the high school had won. Mrs. Pope reminded me that I had been especially attentive that week (a rarity for me), so she had selected me for this special task. I felt on top of the world. But she solidified my place when she told me (in front of the class) that I could choose one other person to go with me. I don't think I touched ground for a week. Customer love can work the same way. The wise service provider helps customers discover their power in special ways.

DELIGHT ME

It goes by many handles—delight, dazzle, and knock your socks off. Regardless of the qualifier, *service with surprise* still tugs at the heartstrings of most customers. We cannot rely on "wowing" the customer as our mainstay; at some point, we run out of room in trying to one-up the last experience. None of our long-term relationships can hang on perpetual delight. Still, most of us still enjoy an occasional, unexpected gesture or the thrill of making a moment. Delighting customers is still a key part of the anatomy of love.

A key advantage of dealing in delight is what it does to the front-line person. Such as in planning a surprise birthday party, the creators gain as much as the recipients. The pursuit of enchantment helps associates think differently about customers. Connections are more personal; communications more attentive. When associates are part of a culture that supports customer delight, there is a sense of joy that is passed on to customers, who reciprocate with their affirmation, gratitude, and loyalty. The cycle repeats, and all players are bolstered.

BE PATIENT WITH ME

I recently bought a television that was DVD compatible. Now, I know about as much about electronics as my cat, Taco. I went to the local TV store and asked for an expert on TVs. It was late in the day and right before a holiday. The store was packed.

"What is DVD?" I asked. The salesperson gave me the third-grade answer, which was the level of complexity I needed. "Can I get a TV that will do DVD at some point in the future, but not be a DVD TV?" (The DVDs cost almost as much as my house!) Again, he gave me a simple, but thorough answer. At this point, there were six customers waiting to be served; they overheard some of his answers and figured he was their guy as well.

Three hours later (it wasn't really that long, but it probably seemed that way to him), I gave him my credit card and made arrangements for the new TV to be put in my car. Was the salesperson enthusiastic? I would call him focused. Was the salesperson highly personal? I would call him highly competent. Would I go back for a repeat? You bet! He earned my loyalty through his insistence on hanging in there with me to the end. He never gave up, never revealed the slightest exasperation, never let anything distract him from his mission of insuring I got precisely what I needed and wanted.

Customer love is not always fancy, sparkly, or emotionally charged. Sometimes it is ordinary and pedestrian. The capacity to give and take is a virtue of all important relationships. Just as there is a dark side to "for better" and "in health" in life relationships, customer relationships also have their ups and downs. Customers do not expect you to be perfect. In fact, if you are perfect they begin to question your capacity to grow and change. They do expect you to care. How service providers demonstrate that caring can make a major difference in the adoration of those served.

BE GENEROUS

This is the era of the short term. We expect results to happen faster and faster. The taxi does not go fast enough, the stock market is not open long enough, the sales graph is not steep enough. The frenetic raising of all standards evokes a greed mentality. "How can I help?" has been too often replaced with "What have you done for me lately?" We think far more about squeezing margins than we do about extra helpings.

Customers adore service providers who are not preoccupied with keeping score. Such service providers know that generosity works like love—the more you give, the more there is. The "giver" mentality is what makes marriages work, partnerships prosper, and customers fall in love. The wisdom of generosity lies in its being laced with authenticity. That suggests a culture where associates are treated with the same abundance they are encouraged to demonstrate to customers.

These are the parts of customer love. But they are good "just for today." Remember my dart board analogy. What gets you points today may not even be on the board tomorrow. And the part that hit my bullseye may be as different from yours as Mutt and Jeff's view of Mutt's wife. What will be important in gaining and sustaining customer love will be the effective use of tools like dramatic listening and displays of empathy.

3
CUSTOMER LOVE: UNWRAPPED

Mrs. Ashley was the supreme commander and only staff member of the Telfair County High School library in my rural South Georgia hometown. She seemed to work around the clock to make the library "the place to be." When I worked closely with Mrs. Ashley on our school newspaper (she was the adviser), I once asked, "Mrs. Ashley, why do you work so hard to make the library special? It's not like you have any competition." It was the early 1960s. I was taking civics and anxious to show off what I'd learned about the workings of business enterprises.

"Oh," she said, "but I *do* have competition. The newsstand at the McRae Pharmacy is one of my competitors. You know, they have far more comic books, and a soda fountain to boot!" She continued, "Besides, a lot of the books I have here are also in the public library. I want students to choose this school library because of the way you are treated, not because we have great books." Mrs. Ashley loved students, and she loved serving them.

At our last class reunion, my classmates and I talked a lot about the impact Mrs. Ashley had on our lives. (She is currently shelving books in that great library in the sky.) The most poignant comment came from a classmate who went on to become a college professor. "Even then," he said, "she treated me like the person I was going to become, not the person she saw in her library. She truly loved her opportunity to make a difference."

Organizations famous for attracting customer love can tell you there is no correlation between just satisfying the customer and earning customer devotion. If not satisfaction, what causes customers to demonstrate loyalty? Sometimes great service reviews come from a single, extraordinary, dazzling service experience. But pursuing the "exceeding customer expectations" trail can be problematic. Customer allegiance will abide only as long as dazzlement happens often enough. And perpetual dazzlement, while a great goal, is not likely to be sustainable. Sooner or later, you run out of room. The long-term allegiance is more likely to come from a feeling of devotion—love.

Mrs. Ashley had a love-driven library. She loved students more than tidy book shelves and "you could hear a pin drop" quietness. She loved kindling an interest in reading far more than maintaining up-to-date card catalogs and mannerly study halls. But how do you create a love relationship with customers? Mrs. Ashley did a lot to make many of us "fall in love with the library."

STEP 1: SHE GOT HER CUSTOMERS INVOLVED.

Mrs. Ashley had a lot of helpers—more than any teacher in the school. And the tasks she delegated were far more than "dust the eraser" chores. We were asked to do more grown-up stuff—like calling the interlibrary loan headquarters on behalf of the school, writing the application for the school to be represented at the state essay contest, or doing research for the editor of the county newspaper. And she always made requests (not demands) in an adult-to-adult manner. You not only felt special, you felt special and grown-up.

STEP 2: SHE CONNECTED WITH HER CUSTOMERS.

Mrs. Ashley was a tiny woman with a kind of withered look about her—like she had washed her face too hard for too long. But she also had a surprising smile, one that got aimed at you when you least expected it. Most teachers sat at their desks and did busy work as students came and went from their rooms.

Mrs. Ashley was a greeter. She "managed by walking around" long before Tom Peters coined the phrase. She was also a toucher. Left shoulder pats were her specialty. A normally noisy troublemaker got a shoulder pat when *he* (and they were all *hes*) was particularly quiet for an unusually long time. The library reflected her disposition—warm, approachable, and focused. There was no other place at school where you almost felt at home, except maybe the playground.

STEP 3: SHE WAS A GENTLE MENTOR TO HER CUSTOMERS.

Peggy Marion and Alan Ryles courted all the way through high school. Peggy was a natural-born scholar; Alan was a natural-born juvenile delinquent. Except for "The Park," the school library seemed to be their favorite spot for intimate conversation. Not that they talked out loud; they just wrote a zillion notes to each other during study hall in the library.

Alan had an antique Renault (named the "Roachy Bug"), which he spent hours underneath. Mrs. Ashley never asked the amorous couple to curb their note writing. She would just put the latest copy of *Popular Mechanics* on the table between them, always with a tap on Alan's left shoulder. It channeled his one-track mind from the moment to the morrow.

STEP 4: SHE SHOWED CUSTOMERS THEY WERE TRUSTED.

Trust begins with experience; experience begins with risks. Mrs. Ashley let students experience her trust in them. She eliminated all the library rules and procedures that had a "guilty until proven innocent" theme or tone. She weeded out the ones that "apply to all in order to catch the very few." There was never a "prove it to me first" theme in any of her dealings.

Mrs. Ashley never used controlling language or words that sent an "I don't trust you" message. Students didn't incure "fines"; she called them "extended-use fees." Instead of saying, "You have an overdue book," she would say, in a completely factual tone, "My records show . . . " as if to communicate, "You go check your records, and we'll resolve this like civil people." Instead of chastising shoddy form completion for an interlibrary loan request, she put up a poster educating students on the many people in the chain who must handle each loan request. Students learned why accuracy and completeness are important.

STEP 5: SHE HELPED HER CUSTOMERS FEEL POWERFUL.

Stuart Garrison got $50 for his 18th birthday. Since he was a good friend of mine, I knew it was going to be used on the down payment for an old Ford truck. Well, the money was stolen during third period. Guess where Stuart was during third period? Study hall in the library. It just so happened that we were having a pep rally that afternoon, and Mr. Roundtree used the assembly to chastise students for taking things that did not belong to them—specifically Stuart's money. I remember it like it was yesterday. The following day, Mrs. Ashley announced to the third period study hall that she had told the principal she was absolutely confident that no one in third period had taken Stuart's money. We all felt very valued. It turned out, Stuart had a small hole in his pocket, and the rolled-up $50 bill had fallen down his pant leg into his sock. He got a lesson in forbearance; we got one on allegiance.

STEP 6: SHE ENCHANTED HER CUSTOMERS

Mrs. Ashley was full of surprises and intrigue. She seemed to know every student's favorite author, and many times she would greet a student with an excited, "Look whose new book I just got in today. You can be the first person to check it out." Her enchanting library posters were the talk of the school because they were an early version of *Trivial Pursuit*. Instead of having a poster saying, "Charles Dickens Week," her posters would say, "What did Madame Defarge knit each day?" or "What were Sydney Carton's final words before they whacked off his head?"

STEP 7: SHE MADE SERVICE COMFORTABLE FOR CUSTOMERS.

Mrs. Ashley made getting library service comfortable. Today's customers demand service fast (like Jiffy Lube), easy (like Domino's), around the clock (like Kinko's), and their way (like Burger King). Assemble these ingredients and add a dash of "tender loving care," and you have the makings of memorable service that your customers will rave about. Great service is delivered in a neighborly manner; customers are treated like special friends. The service system—the process customers have to go through to get their needs met—is crafted for the comfort of the customer, not the convenience of the service provider. I remember calling Mrs. Ashley at her home one evening with a last-minute research question. Mrs. Ashley was thrilled that I called!

STEP 8: SHE SHOWED HER CUSTOMERS SHE CARED.

Mrs. Ashley listened *and* acted. Many service providers brag about how well they listen to customers. However, those seeking to attract customer love work to listen in a manner that lets customers know their input is valued and makes a difference. Emphasis shifts from the server's actions to the customer's experience.

Mrs. Ashley frequently asked students what they liked and didn't like. She explained it this way: "The Longhorn Restaurant didn't start carrying onion rings and Dashboard Specials because they read it in a book. They asked the kids who hung out there about likes and dislikes. And I'd like students to cruise the library at least as often as they cruise the Longhorn!"

She gave surveys for homeroom teachers to distribute so students could register their kudos and critiques, wishes and fears about the library. She cornered student leaders to pick their brains. She installed a simple suggestion box in the private study rooms, figuring students would more likely offer ideas unobserved than risk having their buddies label them a "nerd" (we called them "squares" back then). But here's the amazing part:

43

she actually made changes to the library based on what she learned, and she let us know how much she appreciated our ideas. The more impact we had, the more input we gave, and the more interested we became in the school library.

Mrs. Ashley was a pioneer in customer love. Without being mushy, pushy, or buddy-buddy, she lassoed students' hearts through her continuous and quiet focus on them, their needs, and often their unspoken desires. It made her an insider. Every issue of the school newspaper contained juicy tidbits about students that even the most popular kid had not heard. Since I was on the newspaper staff, students would sometimes ask me how Mrs. Ashley knew so much. I did not have a clue—about that or much of anything back then.

The last high school class reunion was a mosaic of tributes that collectively revealed her secret. She let us know she loved us, and we loved her back.

4

INCLUSION: CUSTOMERS CARE WHEN THEY SHARE

"How about going and getting the tractor and parking it in the barn?" These sweet words were music to my ears when I was a 10-year-old growing up on a farm. It was my dad's way of nudging along my maturity. To get the very special privilege of starting, driving, and parking a large, expensive tractor communicated trust and respect. His gesture also left me feeling like a partner.

I have recently reflected a lot on that childhood experience, in part because my dad passed away just a few years ago at age 84. The death of a parent is typically a passage that prompts nostalgia and reflection. But I've been thinking about the incident for another reason. There is a magic that inclusion has on all relationships—especially customers. The tractor-parking incident was more than a badge of being "grown up." It was a symbol of mutual devotion—I obviously relied on my dad, but at that moment, he trusted me enough to return that dependence. Customers who feel loved reward organizations with long-term loyalty.

Inclusion begins by being comfortable enough to ask the customer for assistance. It also means being willing, at times, to sacrifice some efficiency or effectiveness for the commitment gained by inclusion. It would have been safer and perhaps faster for my dad to have parked the tractor in the barn himself. But he opted for partnership over perfection. When customers are invited to assist, the path they take may not be identical to the one you would take or expect. It's the same with effective delegation—the delegator must exchange some control for cooperation.

SEVEN KEY PRINCIPLES OF CUSTOMER INCLUSION

As I reflect on the magic of customer inclusion, I wish to add a few guidelines.

1.Only ask for what is reasonable—a request appropriate to make of a loyal customer. Avoid any customer request that makes the organization or customer in any way liable or puts either at risk if things go wrong. While your goal is to help the customer feel like a member of the family, you need to remember that the customer is always the guest of the organization.

A few years ago, Hurricane Hugo caused an unexpected crowd at Myers Park Hardware in Charlotte, North Carolina, as customers rushed to purchase candles, propane gas, camping stoves, flashlight batteries, and other emergency supplies. The store turned to its patrons for help.

As three frequent customers were recruited by the store manager to assist in bagging merchandise and ringing up sales, the crowd of formerly frustrated customers suddenly broke out in applause. These "volunteers" also registered their pleasure with the scene by offering to give up their "helper" slot to the highest bidder. It became a bit like Tom Sawyer convincing his skeptical on-lookers that whitewashing a fence was an honor only for the carefully chosen and lucky few!

2. Make the request the way your mother taught, using the "may I" and "please" courtesies you learned growing up. Preface your request with a simple statement—"I need your help."—or a simple question—"May I ask a small favor?" Simplicity and sincerity are important tunes and tones to help the customer get with the rhythm of partnership. My dad never barked a "Go get the..." order; rather, his "how about" requests always carried the tone of a partner inviting a partner.

3. Provide customers with brief background information when making a request for assistance. Avoid complaining or whining. Simply and positively describe the reason for your invitation for help. And be clear and specific about how the customer can assist. It might be as simple as: "We are a bit swamped today, and I could really use your assistance. If you could complete your own paperwork on this order while I get the part, I can get you processed and on your way a whole lot faster. What do you think?"

I was enjoying a three-day stay at a Courtyard by Marriott Hotel. Shortly after lunch on my second day, the hotel manager placed a hand-printed sign in the lobby. "Dear guests: We need your help. The aunt of one of our housekeepers passed away and her funeral is this afternoon. Since the aunt was a special person in our housekeeper's life, we all felt we should be at the funeral. There will only be one employee on site, at the front desk, between 2 and 3:30 p.m. We appreciate your understanding. Thanks!"

The Courtyard customers immediately shifted into a mode of helping each other. Customers served other customers coffee in the lobby cafe. Customers greeted arriving guests and personally explained what was on the lobby sign. Customers demonstrated great patience and tolerance. There was a tone of camaraderie that even carried over to the following day.

4. Requests for customer participation must contain the element of choice. The customer must clearly have an option to pass on involvement. Make a customer demand, and you are asking for resistance. Avoid making customers feel "guilted" into meeting your request. Customers made to feel guilty may comply and respond today, but they will quietly disappear tomorrow.

5. Make certain the customer sees participation as a collective effort. The customer must experience your sharing in the effort or he or she will feel duped, set-up, and unfairly used.

Customer participation is a powerful tool for customer commitment. However, remember that the pronoun in power is "we."

6. *Give the customer plenty of breathing room.* This means being selective in how and when customers are invited to participate. Too little participation and the customer never gets to feel the glow of inclusion. But too much participation can be worse—the customer will feel crowded and leave feeling like "They knew me too well" or "They took me for granted." Smother customers and they will fly away; take them for granted and they will steal away in the night without warning.

Several years ago, I was working three or four days of every month in Miami on a long-term consulting project. I chose a comfortable chain hotel within walking distance of the client's headquarters. I got to know everyone in this "home away from home" hotel. They would do small favors for me; I would sing their praises and encourage my client and others to use the hotel for major meetings.

After a year, however, the "shine" wore off, and I began to be treated too familiarly. Employees told me their hard luck stories like I was a fellow employee; one even gave me his resume to help him find another job and leave the hotel. They once gave me a poor room when a large group of executives came in. Their explanation: "We knew *you* would understand and not mind!" They never bothered to ask me ahead of time. The punch line? I plotted my escape and switched hotels for the final 36 months of my Miami work.

7. *Never forget to express your gratitude.* The organization (a.k.a., managers, supervisors, associates) may ask us to do things all day long. To say "thanks" all the time, every time, is unrealistic. However, asking a customer to assist should be as unique as it is special. Customers will remember it that way if you remember to always communicate appreciation for their efforts. Remember, customer requests should be seen as an option for the customer. Reward them for caring enough to accept that option by letting them hear, and feel, your thanks.

A secret to customer loyalty is the magic of inclusion. The wise organization makes the path to customer contribution comfortable and obvious. As you find opportunities for customer inclusion, remember, some customers want to be pampered, not partnered. They would be insulted if you suggested they do more than give you their money.

For customers who would enjoy participation, the trick is finding and maintaining the balance between using the customer and ignoring the customer. Look for your special version of "How about going and getting the tractor and parking it in the barn." Your customer will feel trusted and respected.

5

CONNECTION: THE MAGIC TOUCH OF SERVICE

A large public library in the middle of a large Northeastern city wanted to add a little extra to the service experience of its patrons—a touch. The checkout clerk was instructed to look patrons directly in the eye and make some physical contact as books were being checked in or out—a handshake, a pat on the arm, or a gentle tap on the wrist. But only on Monday, Wednesday, and Friday. On Tuesday, Thursday, and Saturday, there was to be only eye contact. Outside the front door, a researcher was waiting to ask exiting patrons to rate the library on a one-to-10 scale. The Monday-Wednesday-Friday patrons gave the library considerably higher marks than the Tuesday-Thursday-Saturday patrons.

Now, before you rush to some weird conclusion that has your front-line people attending "customer hugging" classes, know that the issue is not about physical contact. It is about connection. People are favorably attracted to service providers when there is an emotional link. And when that link is profound (without being imprudent), congruent (as in not out of place), and uncorrupted (as in truthful and genuine), it becomes part of a memorable attraction. Rollo May wrote, "When we reach out in passion, it is met with an answering passion and alters the relationship forever." While Rollo might have overstated the power of "reach out and 'touch' someone," his point was in the right direction. Emotional connections, done properly, alter or amplify affection.

Once, my wife and I were guests at the legendary Hotel Del Coronado in San Diego. It was a special occasion with lots of planning for the perfect getaway. We checked in during the middle of the afternoon, and the bell man escorted us up to the room. Unfortunately, it was far from the special room we had planned. Sensing our displeasure, the bell man said, "You are not pleased with your accommodations, are you?" I explained that we had prepaid for an oceanfront room with a king-sized bed, not an ocean-view room with two double beds. "Let me see what I can do," he said, "I'll be right back." Minutes later he returned and stated that the front desk clerk had made a mistake. However, the proper room was not yet cleaned. We could either remain in the room for an hour or so and he would return to move us, or we could take a nice walk on the beach and he would move our luggage for us, leaving our new room key for us at the desk for us. We were beginning to feel better about our situation.

That evening we had an elegant dinner in the hotel restaurant. We had been back in our room for only a few moments when there was a knock on the door. It was the same bell man. "I thought you might enjoy a nightcap . . . ," he said as he looked me in the eye and warmly extended his hand, " . . . with our apologies." He had asked the restaurant what before-dinner drinks we had ordered and had them duplicated as our before-bed treat! Now when we think of the Hotel Del, his special gesture is remembered more vividly than the distinctive beauty of the century-old landmark hotel.

What made this incident a customer love producer? I have reflected on it frequently. The bell man *sensed* our displeasure on entering the first room; his antenna was up high as he stayed connected to our non-verbal behavior. He confronted the front desk clerk out of our earshot. Had he used the bedside phone for his "we have a problem" discussion, it might have further intensified our disharmony.

He was boldly truthful about what happened. There were no excuses, no "this was an exception" explanation, no lengthy justifications. He gave us options, and stayed in control of the resolution. Our anxiety was lowered by knowing that he was not delegating the solution, but staying on the case. After all, why bring in another relationship when he was well on his way to bonding with us?

He looked for a personalized solution—one that was congruent with the "romantic" purpose of our stay. Bringing us a coupon for a complimentary future stay or instructing the housekeeper to leave extra mints when she came for turndown service would not have had the same feel as bringing us our special preference in beverages. He was assertive in his apology and authentic in his handshake. Bottom line, what made his gesture attract our love was his special touch—a heart-to-heart connection that communicated, "I care about you, I care about this hotel, and I care about your memory of this experience."

CONNECTIONS MUST BE NOTEWORTHY

Customer connections are about a link, not about contact. They create the bond of love when they stir our emotions, not just get our attention. This means they must be laced with spirit, energy, and attitude. They work when the customer voluntarily responds or is involuntarily moved. This suggests that the connection is out of the ordinary without being out of harmony. If the customer is expecting a smile and gets a smile plus a handshake, you win. But if the smile is coupled with a big bear hug, you will probably not win.

We live in a time when most cultures are diverse. The norms and mores make establishing noteworthy connections something that must be tailored. Gender, race, and age might shape what is workable between connector and connectee. One might hug their mother in almost all cultures. But hugging your drill sergeant or IRS agent during you tax audit might evoke less than an enthusiastic response.

What else makes a connection profound? It is profound when it works. It is profound when it makes you, as well as your customer, smile. It is profound when it makes you, as the service provider, look forward to execution with the excitement of a nine-year-old waiting for Santa. It is profound when the experience bears repeating to others. It is profound when it stays in your memory bank for some time afterward, or when a smile surfaces when the service provider is mentioned.

A Dallas restaurant famous for its lively ambiance and surprising frivolity often has waiters applaud when a repeat customer enters the restaurant. That might be an embarrassing gesture at a four-star, fancy place, but it fits well with the wildness of Celebration West. St. Luke's Medical Center in Milwaukee asks patients to name their favorite flower. When a patient comes to the hospital again, they are presented with a single stem of that flower. The 40-cents-a-stem cost pales in comparison to the devotion created by the acknowledgment.

CONNECTIONS MUST BE CONGRUENT

The customer connection must make sense in its context. Stated differently, it must fit. A complimentary bottle of champagne at a fast food restaurant would be as dissonant as a free serving of french fries at a four-star restaurant.

However, a congruent connection is more than matching bond with backdrop, or affirmation with ambiance. It must be congruent with tone and style. As a former service quality instructor at the Disney Institute put it, "Disney makes magic with pixie dust. Whatever they do smells right, tastes right, sounds right, as well as *feels* right. Bottom line, it is theatrically pure."

Connections attract customer devotion when they are theatrically pure. American Airlines has turned many frequent business travelers from mild supporters to passionate devotees through their executive platinum desk. Accessed only by their most frequent travelers, the team of helpers is staffed by American's very best. As world-class problem solvers, the helpers delight in surprising their patrons with their capacity to work miracles. Their confident, warm style is often a great relief to the tired traveler caught with an unexpected layover in Peoria and no way out until morning.

Once I was working in downtown Denver. Through the local hotel, I arranged for a driver to take me to the Denver International Airport for my 8:45 p.m. (and last) flight to Dallas. As I waited in the hotel lobby for the tardy driver, I began to worry that I might not make the flight. I called the executive desk to inquire about alternate routing or the availability of a seat on the 6:45 a.m. flight the next morning. The upbeat helper (Jane) asked my location and requested I hold for a couple of minutes. Then, she came back on the line to inform me that a Lincoln Town Car would be at the hotel within five minutes to transport me to the airport, and while it would be close, I should make my flight.

The story does not end there. When the driver arrived, I was impressed, but not "in love." Twenty minutes later, Jane had gotten my cell phone number and called to advise me that the flight was delayed 30 minutes and I would make it alright. And there's more. When I boarded the flight, I was informed by the flight attendant that Jane had called and requested that they take very good care of me on the Denver-Dallas flight, that I had been through a few challenges in making the flight.

Every step she took was more than value-added. Each act built on the last. Each was another step up. And each fit perfectly. They were theatrically pure. I needed a problem solver who cared, not a free drink. I needed follow-up and information, not a coupon for a discounted fare. She was always warm, never coy. She gave me confidence through her professionalism, not her wit.

Customer connections work when they are in sync with the dream of the service receiver. You might get a connection you never expected, but it should always be a connection that, on reflection, has you say, "That made sense."

CONNECTIONS MUST BE UNCORRUPTED

"One of the surest signs of a bad or declining relationship with a customer is the absence of complaints. Nobody is ever *that* satisfied, especially not over an extended period of time. The customer is either not being candid or not being CONTACT-ED." These words of Harvard professor and marketing guru Ted Levitt were tucked in his classic *Harvard Business Review* article, "After the Sale is Over."

His message worried me for days. Here I was striving to minimize customer irritation and ire only to have Levitt tell me that no COMPLAINTS was something to be avoided, and it was my fault for not getting any. I was confused. Weren't we supposed to be seeking all A's, zero defects, 100 percent, five-stars, a hole-in-one? How can "getting more customer complaints" be a virtue? Can you imagine marching into the boss with the "good news" that complaints were up 23 percent, and therefore you needed a bigger budget, more staff, and a large salary increase?!

Then, I had one of those significant emotional experiences with my wife of 35 years. We were attending a weekend retreat associated with our son's school—sort of a family enrichment workshop. One assignment was for each of us to write a list of the strengths and limitations of the other members of the imme-diate family.

My wife and I enjoy a very open, honest partnership. Yet the pace of managing dual, fast-paced professional careers with typ-ical family challenges can work counter to the late-at-night, no-kid-gloves honesty we desire. When she read my limitations out loud ("You sometimes focus so totally on your work that we don't get the attention we need" or "You go into too much detail"), it had a rather sobering effect on me. The exercise pro-voked a level of candor we'd not had in a while.

I began to appreciate why Levitt compared a quality customer relationship with a marriage. "The sale consummates the courtship, at which point the marriage begins. The quality of the marriage depends on how well the seller (and service person) manages the relationship," wrote Levitt. "The absence of candor reflects the decline of trust and the deterioration of the relationship." The key to having customers feel like advocates for and partners with your organization is the quality of their communication with you.

My weekend encounter prompted me to examine other components of customer partnership and long-term loyalty. Customers, like spouses, do not expect us to be perfect; they just expect us to show that we care enough to strive to improve. When we demonstrate caring, customers reciprocate by caring enough to offer their feedback and suggestions. My wife's cataloging of my improvement opportunities was not an act of critical judgment, but rather an act of caring, loyalty, and, love.

Connections work when they are clean—laced with integrity. *Clean connection* means honesty. It also means genuine. A strong connection that the customer recalls as contrived and phony creates disdain and suspicion, not faith and love.

E. M. Forster wrote in his classic, *Howard's End*, "Only connect." It was an invitation to rely on the power of focus, the gift of care, and the joy of mutuality. Customers accelerate their ardor from the transience of "I shall return" to the permanence of "I do" when their union with a service provider touches their soul and not just their assets.

6

ENLIGHTENMENT:
GROWING CUSTOMER LOVE

Larry Leaman is a full professor of customer service! From him I have learned how to cut mailing costs and increase my administrative efficiency. He has tutored me through many classes on ways to keep my clients better informed on the benefits I could provide. He mails me educational flyers and shares with me innovative ideas on marketing—ideas that helped his business, and, he believes, may benefit mine.

Larry teaches at no university. He is neither consultant nor advisor. He is the manager of the Eagle Postal in Dallas, Texas, near my office. Ostensibly, Larry handles my packaging, shipping and bulk mailing. But he gives me much more. He latchkeys my loyalty through his perpetual efforts to make me smarter. He is my customer service mentor—and one of the best.

As automation and labor-saving breakthroughs increase the potential for our lives to be more leisurely, they also make them more complex. Few people would say they work less today than 10 years ago, despite the promises of futurists a few years ago. As our productivity has grown, we have added more activities to fill the hole created. This means smartness has become a prerequisite for success. Brains have not only replaced brawn in the world of enterprise; the half life on knowledge (that time line between when we acquire a skill and when that skill is obsolete) has made continuous learning a key to survival.

Wise customers seek learning in practically every facet of life. We want software that not only instructs in application but offers insights into possibilities. When products come with assembly instructions, we also want to know about maintenance, add-on features, and access to information on upgrades. Call center employees get dinged by customers much faster for inadequate knowledge than for rude interchange. In fact, we'd rather have a surly expert than a polite idiot.

There are customers who enjoy learning for learning's sake. A few are not particularly concerned with applying or using new knowledge or skill—the process of acquiring it is their solitary goal. I had a political science professor who saved up his sabbaticals until he was 71. Then he took three years off and went to law school. Graduating number one in his class, he returned to his teaching post for one year and retired at 75. What was Dr. Saye's motivation? He was simply turned on by the process of learning.

But most customers are not Dr. Saye's. Most see learning as a necessity, not a benefit. Some recall early learning experiences as less than positive. Some don't want to be bothered with the time it takes for instruction. As one person said, "If proficiency in life required reading a manual, I'd flunk out tomorrow."

While "tutor me or lose me" is not yet the by-word of today's customer, smartness is fast become a service expectation. And the service provider able to implant enlightenment into the experience will win customer devotion. The infusion of growth into the service can effectively be achieved through one of three ways: as a natural extension, a delightful addition, or a hidden benefit.

THE EXTENSION: FROM INSTRUCTION TO INSIGHT

A health care client asked me to help obtain 360-degree feedback for their top 100 managers. Each manager wanted input from his or her boss, all subordinates, six peers, and six employees further down in their organizations—about

2,000 lengthy questionnaires. Normally, I'd have roughed out an instrument and subcontracted the entire MIS part to a firm that specialized in survey research who would have crafted a computer program, input the data with a pricey scanner, and returned to me 100 computer printouts neatly tabulated… along with a handsome bill.

The challenges of managed care have put new restrictions on this particular client, and they requested a bargain basement approach. It meant finding a computer process I could create which enabled a clerk to manually input the data and have my laptop computer crunch the numbers and print out the data. Apian Systems came to the rescue.

Apian Software provided an inexpensive software program called SurveyPro. The manual was imposing. Besides, computer manuals are to me one notch above a root canal on the pain scale. But I loaded the program, and the tutorial program literally talked me through the process. When I got stumped, I appealed to Apian tech support to find me a local person who knew the software so I could hire him or her to do my part.

"Oh, no you don't," said the extremely warm tech support person. "You don't want to miss out on this fun. Besides, I will be here to help you when you need me. Why don't you e-mail me what you've done so far, and we can figure out what to do next." I was back to my laptop feeling a bit better and willing to go again at unraveling my puzzle. After two phone calls and three e-mail notes, I had a terrific-looking survey. It wasn't until a colleague asked for some help on a survey that I realized the enormous amount of survey research knowledge the tech support person had subtly implanted in me.

How did she make my learning experience a natural extension? First, she focused on discovery, not answers. Whatever step was taken, I not only learned how and why, I was indirectly given a key to a higher lever…as in, "If it will do this, I bet it would also do that." She delivered far more questions than statements, facilitating my thinking and understanding, not just my response. She continually encouraged me by reminding me of how far I had come. She never used jargon, never exhibited impatience, and never sounded patronizing. And she followed up with important updates that built on my knowledge gradually. At no point was I overwhelmed or overtaxed. She helped me learn through simply doing the program.

A DELIGHTFUL ADDITION: PUZZLES INTO PLEASURES

"Just a spoonful full of sugar makes the medicine go down" suggests the popular song from the movie *Mary Poppins*. It telegraphs a philosophy long used by stern mothers with cranky kids, clever teachers with reluctant pupils, and wise organizations wishing to build customer devotion. When we make learning a delightful addition to the service experience, we create a memory that attracts customer loyalty.

When the day came for the cost of a first class stamp to go from 32 to 33 cents, I was prepared. Not because I read about the change-over day from the news; Larry Lehman reminded me of it in a delightful manner. He sent me a reminder letter a few days beforehand and enclosed a sheet of one cent stamps. I changed my postage machine, ordered new stamps and increased my loyalty to his Eagle Postal Center.

Vivian Carroll is my world-class stockbroker. When I elected to go on-line to track my investments, she sent me the Merrill-Lynch On-Line CD along with my secret access code to my account on the Merrill-Lynch web site. Then she called (I live in Dallas, and she's in Charlotte, NC). "When you get ready to use it, call me at home," she said. "We'll each fix an adult beverage, and I'll walk you through the process." She turned pain into pleasure with her strategy. No phone interruptions, no hurried dialogue because the market just made a big change, just focus, entertainment and enlightenment.

The key secret to making learning fun is to engage the customer in a partnership. Think of the process as a reciprocal learning experience. Vivian and Larry both gave me the impression they were learning from my reaction...like, "this is something new I am trying, and you can teach me a lot by letting me know how it works for you." The day after 32 cents became 33 cents, Larry asked: "Did you get the stamps? Was that a helpful reminder? Should I do something like that again in the future?

Delight works best when it surprises...but does not stun. As customers, we like to be charmed; we don't like to be startled. Make it too silly and the customer will discount it. Make it too wild and the customer will see it as pure serendipity and not likely to be repeatable. Make it too personal and the customer will take his or her anxiety and apprehension to your competitor.

THE HIDDEN BENEFIT: HARD-WIRED INTELLIGENCE

We are on the edge of the "smart everything" era. Our automobiles tell us when to change the oil; our on-line grocery store suggests we check our stock of condiments ("You should be almost out of salt"), and our desktop computers cue us when our mother-in-law's birthday is approaching. Hotels remember our preference for pillows, pizza deliverers remember our preferred toppings, and express mail deliverers know right where we leave the package for pickup. Before too long, our refrigerator will be asking our microwave "what's for dinner?" and our air conditioner will tell our tub to "start a hot bath" when our approaching vehicle tells them all we are en route home.

As customers come to anticipate learning components "built-into" products, they will extend that expectation to include all facets of the customer encounter. Wise organizations will insure "smartness" is subtly woven into the fabric of their offering. This means thinking about the customer encounter from the inside out, not just the outside in. A magazine ad for *myCIO.com* depicts a baseball on the living room floor with a cracked window in the background, obviously the aftermath of some neighborhood little leaguer's home run. The caption reads, "What if the baseball could repair the window?" It reflects the "inside out" thinking needed to imbed learning into the service experience.

Larry noticed that I had mailed several items over a two-month period to my publicist, Tammy Richards. "Why don't I have you a rubber stamp made with her name and address," he said. "It'll save you time, and I can do it in your same type style." His special "attention to detail" feature did not stop there. He went back to all my mailings for the previous year, ascertained the high-frequency items, calculated the time it took for me to type mailing labels, and suggested I have four more rubber stamps made. "These are the ones that will be cost effective for you to have done and use," he advised. It was "smart service" at its best. But it gave me an added bonus: it heightened my awareness of wasted efficiency in my consulting practice and provided a new way of thinking that would cause me to discover other drains on office productivity. Larry's lessons subtly contained hard-wired payoffs for my business!

We live in chaotic times. Massive change makes life seem like a roller coaster out of control. While we enjoy a certain amount of diversity and newness, too much leaves us overwhelmed and troubled. We worry about getting behind and not being able to catch up. And "becoming obsolete," both professionally and personally, has a dramatic impact on our livelihood and our lives.

Customers are increasingly drawn to service providers who work as hard to help customers keep up as they do in their own efforts to modernize. Contemporary marketplace reality dictates that those relationships that learn together, earn together. The champions in the new economy will be like Larry Leaman ... adding customer skill to customer service.

7

TRUST: AFFIRMING A COVENANT WITH CUSTOMERS

Have you ever tried to arrange a complimentary dinner delivered on credit to someone in another state? The experience starts with a long-distance call and ends with a lot of disappointment. You're left wishing L. L. Bean, Land's End, and Amazon.com all had food divisions and delivered.

But I'm ahead of myself. It had been a dreary January week for my Minneapolis partner. The post-holiday blues had collided with his year-end paperwork to leave him with less than a cheery disposition. "Why not treat him to a restaurant-quality, 'top of the line' pizza, delivered to his doorstep," I thought, still basking in the seasonal spirit of giving—and the more forgiving Texas climate.

I telephoned Minneapolis information and talked the operator into giving me a list of restaurants in my partner's neighborhood. I called the first, started my story, and was quickly treated to a terse, "Naw, we don't deliver." As I listened to the premature dial tone, I found myself thinking, "I never even got to tell him the 'I'll pay you $100,000 to deliver it' part!"

Two food establishments later, the no-delivery refrain had changed tune to, "Sorry, that's outside our delivery range." Three establishments after that, I was getting, "We could do that, but we don't take credit cards." My Good Samaritan gesture was starting to become expensive, with seven Texas-to-Minnesota phone calls and still no pizza delivery possible. Then

I reached Ben James at Gina Maria's in Excelsior, and my belief in the spirit of service was quickly renewed.

Ben patiently listened to my goal and string of disappointing, long-distance encounters. "You're calling from Texas?" he asked in disbelief. "Well," he said, "we don't take credit cards either, but I trust you. Give me your order, I'll call your partner to arrange for a convenient delivery time, and you can mail me a check." And—this is the best part—Ben even called me back 10 minutes later (long distance on *his* nickel) to let me know that he'd tried my partner's phone number, gotten no answer, and would continue trying. "He may get his pizza tomorrow, but I won't let you down," he said with a smile in his voice.

I sat back in awe. What had made this encounter so special? What was it that made me gladly say, "Ben, you've been so helpful that I'll be adding an extra-special tip to your check. Would you mail me your menu so I can use your services again?" It was not his responsiveness, warmth, or understanding, though they helped. My feeling of being served above and beyond was bound up in his friendly assertion, " . . . but I trust you."

You may be thinking, "This sounds wonderful for small enterprises, but such customer faith wouldn't work with the financial challenges of our organization." However, L. L. Bean's success is tied to faith in customers, and they're far from small potatoes. And when a customer has a problem with a computer purchased from Dell Computer, the $18+ billion-in-revenue company sends the customer a replacement, a program to move files from the old to the new computer, and mailing labels to send back the defective computer. How many organizations would manage the return process the other way around—"Send us the computer and then . . . "? Winning organizations bet on the long-term relationship and demonstrate trust.

Amazon.com has been a phenomenon in the world of e-commerce. When they elected to launch their new online auction service, they sent a letter to all Amazon.com customers. A portion of the letter from CEO and founder Jeff Bezos read:

"We're doing something unusual with Amazon.com Auctions, and it's one of the bolder things we've done: we're guaranteeing buyers a safe auction experience—and we're doing it on the honor system. I need to back up and explain. The vast majority of sellers are honest and faithful, but, with millions of sellers, there are bound to be a few losers—frauds who take your money and don't ship the promised items. Fraud will be rare, but the Amazon.com Auctions Guarantee means that if it does happen to you, it's *our* problem. We've made the process as simple as possible. Essentially, we're going to take your word for it if you're ever the victim of fraud."

Trust doesn't begin with "kept promises"; it starts with a leap of faith. Someone takes a risk that builds experience, which leads to trust. And when an organization takes a risk with customers, customers typically respond in kind, and their loyalty soars. Here are five things you can do to build trust . . . and loyalty.

Five Trust Builders

1. Don't step over dollars to pick up pennies. The trusting organization generously puts more focus on nurturing the relationship than miserly squeezing every dollar out of every transaction. This doesn't mean "giving away the shop." Everyone in the organization should protect and grow the assets of the organization. However, customers remember organizations that refrain from "nickel and diming them to death." Look for opportunities to say "No charge" or "That one is on us." Find ways to do little extras for customers that they didn't expect. The small, personalized extras gain more loyalty mileage than big, splashy ones.

Delbert Litchfield is a sea-wall and boat-house builder on Cedar Creek Lake in East Texas. The month after we purchased a weekend lake house near Gun Barrel, we asked different people in the area to recommend a good builder to construct a large boat house. It seemed like Delbert was clearly the neighborhood boat-house builder of choice. So we summoned Delbert.

He arrived the same day we inquired about a bid. We spent an hour or so going over the details—a 75-foot ramp, an electric boat lift, a side platform for diving and swimming, extra electric outlets, spot lights, etc. He took lots of notes and drew rough diagrams. Then he did all his calculations, including his profit, in clear view, leaning over the hood of his truck. He finished and rather proudly announced, "$10,000.00 on the nose!" What was actually showing in the tiny window of his calculator was "$10,236.85."

"Do you need an advance payment or a deposit," I asked this weather-worn stranger, fully expecting the contract part of the conversation to crank up. "Naw," he drawled. "Not until you tell me you are happy with it. Besides, I know where I can find you!" He half-grinned, winked, and turned off his calculator. We agreed he would begin work in a week to finish in three. "Do you need anything?" I asked, still waiting for some catch in this "you don't know me from Adam" leap of faith he was taking. "Yep, two things," he replied, still amused at my citified caution. "Take care of the paperwork with the Cedar Creek Lake Conservation Office. They're gonna want a $50 check. And pray for sunny weather!" I almost missed the last part as he drove into the Texas sunset.

2. *Declare a 60-day trust period.* Be on the lookout for areas where a "We don't trust you" message is being sent to customers. Hold meetings to identify areas needing improvement. Then, separate those areas where legal or quasi-legal issues keep you from changing your practice. With the areas left over, outline new "trusting" steps for everyone to take. At the end of the 60-day period, interview a few regular customers and get their reactions. Keep the changes that customers enjoyed and that you know will make a difference in long-term loyalty.

3. *Consider and pilot test a service guarantee.* Service guarantees can have a powerful impact on the customer's view of trust. Pick areas where you can say to the customer, "If you're not happy, the work is on the house—no forms, no hassles, no red tape." Be sure to guarantee areas customers care about. And select that part of your service that could have an easy-to-explain guarantee. Guarantees that are hard to understand or administer don't send the message you want. Service guarantees need to have no "fine print" and need to be easy for the customer to collect on (no "We'll mail you a check in 90 days"). Service guarantees might be as simple as, "We promise you won't have to wait longer than 10 minutes, or we'll take 10 percent off your service bill." Pilot test guarantees for a limited time or for a portion of your business and see what you learn.

4. Find areas to dramatically demonstrate a trusting attitude. The waiters or waitresses at Vincenzo's Ristorante in Omaha, Nebraska, greet patrons at their table with a pitcher of "honor wine"—an excellent Chianti. "Enjoy this if you like," a waitress said to a group of us recently. "We charge by the glass. At the end of the meal, just let me know how many glasses you had and I'll add it to your bill." When I asked the owner on our way out how many patrons drink the Chianti, he smiled and said, "Most. It's one of our best features!"

Trusting actions can be as small as the cup of pennies next to the cash register. Put a sign on the cup which reads, "Got a penny, give a penny; need a penny, take a penny." My dry cleaner has a sign on his wall that says, "We DO take personal checks." Examine the signs around your organization that say "Don't," "No," or other negatives. Can the same message be communicated in a positive, more trusting way?

5. Trust your associates more. Trusting customers starts with trusting associates, especially since associates are customers as well. Customers like dealing with empowered employees. In fact, customers believe the attitude of the entire organization is reflected in the authority given the front line. If they deal with employees who seem to be untrusted by the organization, they assume they will be treated the same. Examine rules and procedures to isolate those with a "guilty until proven innocent" theme. Rewrite or weed out those that "apply to all to catch the few."

The magical power of trust is that it creates more—show trust to customers, and they'll trust you more. And trusted customers spend more, are more forgiving of mistakes, and champion you more to others. Remember, there is no sweeter sound to a customer than, " . . . but I trust you."

8

BETRAYAL: DEALING WITH OUR OWN GUILT

Customers do not expect organizations to provide perfect service. Now, before you lower your service standards, know that frequent foul-ups will lead to a fast exit for customers. And with the growing number of organizations closing each year, customer loyalty is not only important to success, it's critical to survival.

If you handle service failures effectively, you can turn an "oops" into an opportunity. Research shows that customers who have had their sales or service problem spectacularly solved wind up more loyal than customers who have never even had a problem. How come?

Customers are becoming more insistent on sales and service laced with trust. Dr. Leonard Berry of Texas A&M University has probably done more sales and service research on this than anyone. His research findings show that of all the qualities customers expect—accuracy, responsiveness, or empathy—they value reliability the most. As a customer, reliability means, "Can I trust you to do what you say you will do?" Service recovery is about restoring customers' trust and confidence after a service failure has left them disappointed or angry.

When a customer has a disappointing experience with a producter service, the first service goal is to return that customer back to normal. But how do you heal a broken relationship? How do you effectively handle betrayed trust? What steps work best in providing spectacular recovery?

71

First, think of service recovery as an opportunity to restore trust and build loyalty. Customers who have never had a sales or service problem are uncertain as to how you might handle it. However, if you provide great recovery after a customer has been disappointed, you renew their faith in you. When they see you shine at your darkest hour, customers end up with *more* confidence, not less. More customer confidence leads to greater customer loyalty. And more loyalty leads to customers who buy more, forgive more, and tell others about you more.

HEALING CUSTOMERS

The key to converting a livid customer into a loyal customer lies not in "buying" back devotion ("How about I give you . . . your money back? A free car? A trip around the world?"). Sure, some symbol or gesture of sorrow can help. But the key to recovery is the way you manage the communication in a HEAL-ing manner.

Step 1: Show Humility. Healing communication begins with Humility—an expression of authenticity.Never let your customer hear you say, "We're sorry." Apology should always be delivered in first-person singular—"I'm sorry." "I'm sorry" doesn't suggest you caused the problem, or that you're automatically the culprit. "I'm sorry" means "I care." Obviously, the tone you use to communicate is important. You don't want the customer to hear "I'm sorry" as meaning, "I'm about the sorriest thing on the face of the globe!" Even apologies need to be communicated with confidence.

Lower your voice. Let the customer witness your genuine concern. Always look the customer straight in the eye. Be forthright and direct. There's no need for a "tail between your legs," cowering-down style. Things went wrong; the customer was disappointed. Acknowledge it honestly and frankly, and be ready to learn from it and move on.

Step 2: Express Empathy. Healing communication includes expressions of Empathy—words and actions that let customers know you appreciate their pain, plight, and predicament. It does not mean service people have to wallow in bad feelings. Empathy communicates understanding and identification. Again, just as customers expect caring, they also prefer confidence.

There is an old saying that goes, "You're not qualified to change my view until you first demonstrate you understand my view." Whether you like or disagree with the customer's view is not the point. The goal is to empathize—to give evidence you understand. Fix your customer before you fix your customer's problem.

Empathy doesn't mean the same as *sympathy*. The word *sympathy* means "shared pain"; *empathy* means "in tune with pain." Customers don't want someone to cry with (shared weakness), they want an understanding shoulder to cry on (the gift of strength). And this doesn't mean badmouthing your organization. When customers hear employees saying, "I know what you mean. I wouldn't eat here either if I didn't work here," they walk away with less than confident feelings about the restaurant. Customers seek someone to value and care about their concerns. Remember, the customer's orientation when things go wrong is this: "I don't care how much you know until I know how much you care." Show you care.

Step 3—Exhibit Agility. Healing communication includes Agility—words and actions that tell customers they're dealing with someone who has what it takes to correct their problem. They want can-do competence, attentive urgency, and take-charge, "I'll turn this around" attitudes. Service failure first and foremost robs the confidence customers have in an organization. But that confidence can be restored if customers observe your agility in quickly and confidently implementing a solution to their problem.

The secret to this second step is letting the customer see your efforts. Simply telling a customer, "Wait in the reception area, and I'll work on it." may seem like a polite approach. But it strips the customer of the chance to see you in action. Let the customer hear you call someone and say, "George, we have a problem we need to work on immediately." Let the customer see you walk faster, move more quickly, act more concerned. Remember, confidence is restored by what you do, not by what you promise.

Step 4—Demonstrate Longevity. Healing communication includes Longevity—the after-the-fact experiences of the customer that say: "We won't abandon you now that we have regained your business." It is the opposite of "taking for granted." It is about continuous care and frequent follow-up. Customer service research shows that follow-up is one of the most powerful steps you can take in cementing a long-term relationship, especially after a problem.

Pick up the phone and call the customer to find out if everything is back to normal. Send the customer a note. When the customer returns for future service, ask about the last problem. If customers know you remember and are still concerned, they'll come to realize their bad experience was an exception. And don't forget to follow up with your associates and manager so that whatever caused the problem can be corrected. This way, other customers won't be disappointed.

We are approaching a time when "exceeding customer expectations" is no longer the ticket to success, but to survival. The challenge in all relationships is that exceeding expectations or delight is a far easier goal than maintaining the daily standard. If it wasn't, most of us would not have stayed married much past our honeymoons!

Mistakes are a part of all relationships—with spouses, friends, and customers. However, disappointment can be turned into delight, loss into love by effectively handling service recovery. The best organizations view recovery as an opportunity to heal a broken relationship—through **h**umility, **e**mpathy, **a**gility, and **l**ongevity.

9

Betrayal: Dealing with a Lover's Scorn

"**Y**ou people lied to me!!"

Her biting words bounced off the walls of the customer waiting room. Customers were startled out of their seats. I was one! I thought of that old line: "Hell hath no fury like . . . "

"I am *so* glad you came to *me*," the service person said with noticeable confidence. He moved closer to her and looked her straight in the eye. "Would you be willing to tell me the details?" he said, world-class concern oozing from his voice.

"Mister, I'll tell everybody up your chain of command if I have to." Her junk-yard dog style had bit down on a sympathetic ear, and she was not about to let go.

"I don't want to miss any of this," the service person said, unshaken by her rage. "Could we move in here so I can give you my complete attention?" He ushered her into an office away from the waiting area, and probably away from the object of her irritation.

None of us heard the conversation at the other end of the hallway. Oh, we all talked about his shoes, her loose screw, and his "grace under pressure." Ten minutes later, they emerged from down the hall. "Why can't they all be like you?" were her parting words as the waiting room door closed behind her.

I was lucky. I later got the same service person, which gave me the opportunity to learn of his winning magic.

"It was no big deal," he shrugged. "We all have our bad days, and today was hers. Since she's one of our customers, she deserves my best effort at problem solving." His too-good-to-be-true talent seemed way too special for me to let it go.

"So, you think the customer is always right?" I pressed.

"No," he said, resigning to the fact that he was going to be interviewed. "The customer is the customer—a regular person, right and wrong. They are really no different here than anywhere else in life. Nor am I, to be honest. I try to deal with a difficult customer just like I try to do when my son or wife or neighbor is being difficult."

He handed me my receipt with one last piece of wisdom: "It's all about living with customers as people every day."

Rules for Living

I thought a lot about that waiting room scene. Customers are people with bad days. While there may be "customers from hell"—those evil, rip-you-off types—most customers are far more likely to be "customers who have been through hell." They rant, rave, and raise their voices in embarrassing ways, but mostly they are people just trying to get through life—right and wrong. Coping with difficult customers is just a part of "living with customers as people every day."

Yet, some people are more effective at "living with customers" than others. Some service people get hooked by a customer's rage and end up costing the organization both the customer and a good reputation. Other people seem to be adept at living with customers, especially the testy ones everyone infrequently meets with dread. What's their secret?

I found a unique source of advice on living with difficult customers in a *Peanuts* comic strip. Peppermint Patty asks Charlie Brown: "Chuck, do you know any good rules for living?" And as if he had been for days waiting for that very question, he quips: "Keep the ball low. Always get your first serve in. Always knock before entering. Don't let the ants get in the sugar. Don't spill the shoe polish. Give four weeks notice when ordering a change of address. Don't let your crayons melt in the sun." At this point in the strip, Snoopy appears, lunch pail in his mouth. As Charlie leaves the strip, he gives his final rule: "And feed your dog when he's hungry." Charlie's wisdom is powerful advice for living with difficult customers.

1. "Feed your dog when he's hungry." Customers are obviously not dogs. But Charlie's coaxing us to *urgently* deal with a customer's distress is prudent prose. Making an angry customer wait is like watching an overfilled balloon get more air. While we may be reluctant to oil the squeaky wheel (fearing all wheels will develop squeaks), the price for unrestrained fury can be enormous. Angry customers can make others question their own wisdom in selecting the organization. Unbridled anger takes a toll on the self-esteem of all in its path, especially service people. And customer anger, left unchecked, can turn into "customer terrorism"—that scary realm of lawsuits and trashing the organization in the marketplace. Feed your angry customer's needs when he or she is "hungry."

2. "Always knock before entering." The best antidotes to customer communication challenges are assertive concern and quiet confidence. My front-line service person made three magical moves.

First, he stated, "I am *so* glad you came to *me*." His communication told the customer she had selected the buck-stops-here person. Positive and upbeat, his goal was to make her feel she had hit the jackpot by getting him. He kept his tone confident, but not cocky; he looked concerned, but not delighted. Giving an angry customer a big smile is oil on fire, which customers see as uncaring or patronizing.

Second, he stepped toward the customer. Moving closer creates more intimacy. This is not about getting into uppercut range. Avoid invading the customer's personal space. On the other hand, if you're too far away from the customer to put a hand on his shoulder, you're too removed. The goal is to demonstrate both concern and confidence.

Third, he showed confidence with eye contact and concern by asking, "Would you be willing to give me the details?" Empathy is to communication what knocking on a door is to entering.

3. *"Always get your first serve in."* Tennis players know that missing the first serve adds pressure to the serving process. You pucker up to make the last-chance serve error-free. Communicating in challenging encounters has an even greater pucker factor. Blow your first shot, and you may see your opponent get into position for an overhead smash. You only have one chance to make the right first impression. Take a deep breath when you see rage before you. The added oxygen in your blood stream calms you. Recall a great past success and how you felt—get in the "spirit of greatness." Positive self-talk works as a private half-time pep talk and mentally prepares you to deliver your best. One last thing. Assume this tough customer is your paycheck. How will you treat your paycheck?

4. *"Keep the ball low."* The next step my service person took was to create a change of venue for the angry customer. I suspect he also wanted her out of earshot of other customers. Moving her away from the object of her wrath provided a less volatile setting for her to vent her feelings. Keeping the ball low implies focus and precision. Finding a setting where customers can get undivided attention is a key to unveiling their unspoken issues. This enables you to more precisely find a solution you both can live with.

5. *"Don't spill the shoe polish."* I do not know what tactics he used behind closed doors. But I suspect he worked hard to channel her negative energy toward a solution. It is important to get customers out of a "right or wrong" mode and into a joint problem-solving mode. If the confrontation remains on a "who's right or wrong" plane, you'll lose, even if you win. Never resist resistance. Scenes like this are more like verbal judo than boxing. Flow is more important than force; working with, not working against, is the aim.

6. "Don't Let the Ants Get in the Sugar." Customer fury is always emotional. Your heart (not your head) must speak to their heart. When customers are angry, let them feel your empathy. Be quick to acknowledge their feelings. Be humble, and focus on compassion, not on protection. Be quick to say, "I'm very sorry this happened." Try to stand in their shoes. Ask, "How would you like to see this problem solved?"

7. "Don't let your crayons melt in the sun." Customer fury is rarely personal. Sometimes, intense distress is old negative baggage triggered by a small incident. Customers are sensitive about being betrayed by service providers. They are calloused by too frequent unkept promises, unreliable products, and unbelievable propaganda. Their jaundiced attitudes start them out on the service road with skepticism. One small misunderstanding can unleash a large "I told you so." Consequently, they come ready to do battle with "the whole lot of you." It's usually not about you personally. If you think it is, remember Eleanor Roosevelt's advice: "No one makes you feel inferior without your permission."

8. "Always give four weeks notice when ordering a change of address." Sometimes the best efforts to "soothe the savage beast" are to no avail. Smart organizations devise plans for handling those situations when a service person reaches an absolute dead end. Sometimes it may be finding a different person to serve that customer—a younger or older person, a person of the opposite gender, someone with a different style. It depends on who you think might be a better personality match with the customer. Identify who might be able to get on the right wavelength and save the customer. After the problem is resolved, follow up with the customer to make sure there are no leftover bad feelings.

Charlie Brown's "Rules for Living" can be valuable tools for dealing with those occasional challenging customers. But the *Peanuts* comic strip had one final frame. "Will these rules give

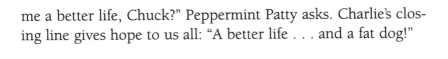

me a better life, Chuck?" Peppermint Patty asks. Charlie's closing line gives hope to us all: "A better life . . . and a fat dog!"

* Quotes from *Peanuts* by Charles Schulz. Reprinted by permission of UFS, Inc.

10

Empowerment: Keeping Customers In Control

Pick your poison: the State Department of Motor Vehicles, the IRS, the U.S. Postal Service, or your doctor's office. We all have been in scenarios where we needed a particular service, we did not have much choice at the time, and we were locked into a process that left us frustrated and angry. When we had absolutely no choice, we took it out on the front-line person. When we had a choice, the service provider who gave us heartburn generally got fired. We not only never came back; we went out of our way to bad mouth them to everyone who would listen.

Recall one of those "I'll never go back there" experiences. What action (or inaction) on the company's part surfaced your momentary consideration of homicide? It was not likely related to some evil act. It was rarely some action that put your finger on the speed dial to your attorney. It was often about the loss of control. We expected an outcome; we were caught in a process that denied us a way to get that outcome in the form or fashion we thought reasonable. And—this is the most important part—we felt victimized and powerless to alter the outcome.

Customer love, just like all forms of love, is about creating a relationship that is power-*full*, not power-*less*. Great relationships are composed of people who feel strong and in control because they are either in control of the outcome or trust the players to take care of them in the process. I cannot control what happens when I go in for a root canal, but I trust my dentist, Charles Bradley, to do what is best on my behalf. I do not feel helpless. In fact, with Dr. Bradley, my dental needs are so effectively managed, I feel more powerful.

CUSTOMER POWER BEGINS WITH "BLESSED ASSURANCE"

Howard Perdue was the owner, manager, and spiritual leader of the Ford Tractor dealership in McRae, Georgia, during the 1950s and '60s. In that region, 185 percent of the population—practically every man, woman, child, dog, horse, and mule—was involved in the overtime occupation of worrying about soybean prices and praying for rain. Since no one could do much serious farming without a tractor and the proper plows, Mr. Perdue was the center of the universe. He was also my mother's brother.

The Perdue-farmer relationship was a special one. Few farmers started the planting season with enough money to fund all their farm equipment needs. They typically bet—along with Howard—on the success of their harvest. Their new tiller, combine, or fertilizer spreader was bought on credit and a promise to pay "when I make my crop." Frequently, farmers had to literally "bet the farm" when an unexpected equipment failure led to a major unexpected expense. But the risk was not only on the customer's side.

My brother, sister, and I would occasionally play among the new tractors in Howard's showroom or chase each other down long aisles of equipment parts. We thought Uncle Howard was a rich man. After all, he owned all this neat stuff! We had no concept of how his livelihood was tied to his customers. If their crops failed, he lost.

Howard's brand of customer love has come to remind me of an old hymn, "Blessed Assurance." One verse of that song, while clearly intending a religious message, implies powerful instructions for how to help customers feel empowered: "Perfect submission, perfect delight, visions of rapture now burst on my sight; watching and waiting, looking above; echoes of mercy, whispers of love."

EMPOWERMENT COMES THROUGH PROMISES KEPT

The Howard Perdue approach to customer love started with a covenant. He would deliver an expensive tractor to a farmer, demonstrating his faith in the customer's ability to "grow" tractor payments. But the farmer had his side of the covenant, too. While "watching and waiting," and "looking above," he relied on the mercy of Howard, the lien holder. If the farmer needed more time to pay, when "we ain't had a drop in weeks," Howard almost always acceded to their wishes. The covenant also contained an unspoken assumption that if all parties were "raptured" by a bumper crop, the farmer would "pay it out early."

Customer empowerment depends on blessed assurance. Assurance begets certainty; it means a guarranty both pledged with conviction and accepted with courage. It is a notice of mutual leaps of faith. It is the "I do" end of the " . . . and thereto I plight thee my troth" promise. Howard's *modus operandi* communicated his belief that "We're in this together."

However, promises must be made in order for promises to be kept. Customer love is never achieved through a "cash and carry only" basis. Promises require acts of courage. The "living trust" dimension of reliability demands actions that give customers an opportunity to demonstrate "perfect submission." As customers, we are empowered by service providers who believe in us and take risks on our behalf.

"The quality of mercy is not strained," said Portia in Shakesphere's *Merchant of Venice*. "It droppeth as the gentle rain upon the place beneath. It is twice blessed. It blesseth him who gives and him who receives." Howard and Portia thought a lot alike.

Parts manager Carl Vardeman, like Howard (perhaps because of him), was more than willing to come down on the empathy side of a hard-luck saga. I once heard him tell an embarrassed farmer pleading his cash-shortage problem, "I'm sure Mr. Perdue will understand your situation. He's back in the garage with Jim; I'll go and get him." I carefully watched from behind the parts counter as Howard emerged from the garage, wiping black engine grease from his hands. The farmer and Howard greeted each other without shaking hands. Farmers generally only shook with the preacher when leaving the church after a good fire-and-brimstone sermon. "How's Mary?" Howard asked, attempting to alter the straight lines on the farmer's despondent face.

I didn't hear the conversation; they went behind closed doors. Mercy giving was always a private affair in those days. But when they emerged, Howard announced to Carl that Mr. Garrison would be getting a new carburetor. It was clearly a coded communication—"echoes of mercy"—a signal from Howard to Carl that credit had been extended, boundaries had been expanded, and trust had been restored. Mercy is marvelous magic. And there was no parting expression of humility from the farmer. Submission had been perfect . . . mutual.

EMPOWERMENT IS ABOUT CUSTOMER AFFIRMATION

I was always surprised by how much Howard seemed to know about his customers. Sure, he had an economic stake in their welfare. But it was more than that. He knew, for instance, that Elmer Peavy made scrimshaw knives, that Daniel Yawn was a crackerjack fly fisherman, and that Lewis Rountree's oldest son was a highly decorated Air Force major. These were facts and fables not gleaned through barber shop talk, the men's Bible class at First Baptist, or the "social" page of the *Telfair Enterprise*. This was knowledge that required precision probing, dramatic listening, and lavish understanding.

Service providers devoted to their customers are not only anxious to learn about their customers, they look for ways to use that knowledge to give the other party public bragging opportunities. Howard did that better than most anyone I know. And the larger the audience standing around the tractor-store showroom, the more assertively he'd ask, "Lewis, is your boy running the Pentagon yet?" Of course, Mr. Rountree would light up the place after such an invitation to play to his favorite topic. And Howard would fire off another "let me pique the curiosity of anyone within earshot" question. The farmers' eavesdropping would soon turn into pumping Lewis for more information. Lewis would emerge as a local hero. Lewis probably plowed his fields more confidently after those encounters.

Part of this ritual was based on sincere curiosity. Howard really *was* interested in the status of Major Rountree. But the larger focus of this ritual seemed to be an act of devotion and admiration. This equation encompassed more than economics; it also contained "whispers of love" and "perfect delight."

Things have changed for the McRae Tractor Company. It is now some other sort of small-town business. Mr. Peavy's eyesight caused him to put up his special knifes, Mr. Yawn's arthritis put a halt to fly fishing, and Mr. Rountree now plows more heavenly pastures.

When I return for visits, I sometimes drive by the old tractor store. Waves of nostalgia take me back to a time when business was almost all about belief in the better side of enterprise. Relationships seemed more revered. Local customers were "for life" deals, like marriages. And even the "just passing through town" customers were treated like neighbors.

Howard Perdue passed away a couple of years ago. He was almost 90. There was standing room only at his funeral, and I was privileged to be one of his pall bearers. At the simple graveside service, a severely stooped, weathered old man came up and asked me questions about how I was related to "Mr. Howard." After I pointed at my mother and clarified the genealogy, he startled me with his comment. "You know," he said, "Mr. Howard was a lot like an old bird dog I had years ago." I politely smiled as if I knew what he meant. Then, he clarified it for me. "He made me feel like the most important and most powerful person in the world." Then he uttered the closest expression of love a South Georgia farmer could pay another: "Mr. Howard was a 'good-un.'"

11

ENCHANTMENT: THE MAGIC OF THE OCCASIONAL MIRACLE

You and I have heard this kind of story many times. Heroic warmth is at its heart. Paul Petrocci's recounting of his story took 500 words on two faxed pages he sent me. "Here's one for your next book," he wrote me in the cover note. I read it, sighed, smiled, remembered, and wished. Now, here is my 90-word version of Paul's story.

Paul had decided to pop *the* question to Adrienne at lunch in the romantic, 10-table loft section of Tucson's Smuggler's Restaurant. The restaurant offered the entire section for the price of his meal and to put "Adrienne, will you marry me?" on their marquee. But when Paul and Adrienne arrived, the staff had gone overboard. Only *his* table remained in the roped-off loft, along with complimentary champagne. For the occasion, the staff had purchased linen, china, silver, and candelabras. His tab: $13; his tip: $150! And Smuggler's made no sales pitch to do his wedding reception. There is much more, but I'm already 10 words past the 90 I promised!

Undoubtedly, you have heard similar stories of sweet, heroic warmth. These *way, way, way* beyond the call of duty stories are generally exotic, extravagant, and frequently involve helicopters, champagne, and penthouse suites. Then, we go back to work thinking, "My boss would kill me if I did something like that." As the cold reality of work quickly freezes out the story's momentary warmth, it gets dropped in our brain's "fairy tale" file.

But is there another side to these enchanting stories? Could extravagant service have a return on investment of size enough to warrant repetition? Should managers challenge their employees to "bring me more lavish bills for unplanned, unbudgeted, red-carpet treatment for customers." In this era of expense control, when waste reduction and downsizing have been more norm than exception, how do you justify an extravagant encounter?

Service extravagance does have an important role in any service-quality effort. Its power, however, lies first in its uniqueness. If you have a steady diet of extravagance, you not only abuse the bottom line, you turn unique into usual—and the magic disappears. For instance, part of the challenge famed retailer Nordstrom faces is that customers have heard so many dazzling Nordstrom stories that they callously walk into a store with an "Okay, I've heard about you people. Let's see you blow *my* mind" attitude. Unrealized expectations, no matter how unfairly inflated, result in customer disappointment. The word is that Nordstrom executives have asked employees to refrain from telling heroic stories to non-Nordstrom audiences.

Having said all that, however, what mileage can an organization gain by "going the extra *10* miles" incidents? Assuming unique is kept unique, there are advantages to encouraging an occasional service extravaganza. While the CFO might have to take a leap of faith, there are great payoffs for service heroics. And service extravagance can foster customer love.

SERVICE EXTRAVAGANCE RELEASES EMPLOYEE POWER

When the subject of empowerment is discussed among a group of leaders, they all lament that employees have far more power and authority than they typically exercise. And it is generally true. Get a group of employees together and they will quickly gripe about their lack of authority. Empowerment (or lack of it) is often code for fear of failure. We all have pent-up memories (of varying degrees) of what happened when we mixed "exacting parent" with "error-prone child."

Celebrating service heroics can encourage employees to "push the edge of the envelope." When their boldness is matched by affirmation, they learn to take risks in other areas. The goal is not to set employees up to get hurt, but rather to encourage them to experience the limits and, if they go too far, learn that the organization's response will be support and coaching rather than punishment and rebuke. Empowerment begins with error; error begins with risks. Employees risk when they believe failure will spark growth, not censure.

A patient at St. Luke's Medical Center in Milwaukee had a favorite pair of sneakers mistakenly discarded by housekeeping. The shabby, worn condition of the sneakers led the housekeeper to conclude that they were surely trash. The upset patient demanded their return. When this proved impossible, the hospital offered to pay the patient for their replacement. But the unhappy patient was not mollified. Another housekeeper, getting a description of the sneakers, left the hospital, went to a nearby mall, and, with his own money, purchased a replacement pair and presented them to the patient. The now elated (and very moved) patient proudly displayed his new sneakers. Not only was the housekeeper celebrated for his service heroics, he became the first recipient of the Golden Sneaker Award, an honor bestowed quarterly on the employee who demonstrates a similar attitude. The incidence of empowered actions at St. Luke's Medical has increased dramatically, altering the entire culture.

Service Extravagance Keeps Service Quality Top of Mind

The challenge every organization faces in creating a service culture is how to keep it new and alive. The early elation of "The Year of the Customer" kickoff quickly turns to exertion when the umpteenth irate customer makes some unreasonable demand on an already exhausted front line. How do organizations ensure that excitement wins out over despair? A part of the answer is to celebrate heroics.

Effective service celebrations begin with "see." The telling of heroic service stories provides a graphic picture of what great service looks like. But too often those witnessing a celebration or the presentation of a service award learn *who* but not *why*. They depart with very little to emulate. And at a deeper level, they never discover the real message. Make certain the story is told in intricate detail, along with the philosophy or attitude demonstrated by the story. People will be reminded of the importance of daily extraordinary service, not the fact that the way to get the big award next year is to send customers home in an unbudgeted limousine because "we screwed up their account."

First Union National Bank, headquartered in Charlotte, North Carolina, holds an annual quality leadership conference in each of the many states in which it operates. Ignoring the time it takes to retell the many stories of the numerous award winners, some conferences spice up the show with slides of the person "in action." At the 1997 Virginia conference, one manager said at the break following a round of awards and stories, "This is a powerful reminder of our core values. When you hear it played out in living color, you not only get a super review, but you get an even more powerful renewal. I'm psyched!'

SERVICE EXTRAVAGANCE BUILDS
TEAMWORK AT ITS BEST

As I read Paul's Smuggler's Restaurant story, I was reminded of my high school class planning the junior-senior prom when we were the 11th grade planners. Now, our class was never known for closeness. We seemed to have more than our share of cliques and conflicts. And we were the class who planned (and was appropriately chastised) for the infamous school-wide lunch room boycott, which caused school principal Elliott Roundtree to completely curtail all privileges and extracurricular activities for the entire school for a few days. As we plotted, planned, and programmed a prom that would be remembered for years as the "party par excellence," a special bond developed that transformed our low class-esteem into a tight family. We had a huge attendance for our 10th , 20th and 30th class reunions.

Service extraordinaire events, when instigated and implemented as a team, can raise morale and reinforce important lessons in interdependence. The adage that "nothing pulls a team together more than a crisis" can be expanded to a "celebration" as well. And since teamwork is a crucial commodity in today's service-sensitive arenas, the winners in the eyes of the customers are less likely to be the single acts of excellence, and more apt to be the collaborative efforts of a collection of colleagues who effectively craft an experience that customers retell over and over. Simply the act alone can fuel teamwork.

So, what do we do with our own organization's version of the story Tom Peters made famous of the Nordstrom customer demanding $200 for tires, or the story Ron Zemke made famous of the FedEx employee who leased a helicopter without permission to get a part to the crew rescuing baby Jessica from the well? We remember that heroics are heroics. We celebrate extravagance as extraordinary. And we work to let employees learn the principle behind the peculiar.

Give elbow room for the exceptional, and your employees will have exciting standards for excellence that can energize them to deliver service performances that customers will remember as special.

12

ELASTICITY: PUTTING STRETCH IN THE RELATIONSHIP

Miss Lena Hartley, bless her heart, was wrong. And she really was trying to be helpful. But sure as rain, she was wrong.

When Nancy Marie Rainey of Walnut Ridge, Arkansas, gave a "yes" answer to my "Will you be my life partner?" question, it was one of the happiest days of my life. But getting married in the Deep South in 1965 was not without challenges. In particular, it required getting the blessing of the guardians of local civility and protocol—the Women's Missionary Circle #4 of the First Baptist Church.

The setting for this important rite was a shower for my bride-to-be, sponsored by the Circle #4. The fact that I was marrying an assertive, razor-sharp Arkansas girl imposed a special inspection requirement on these ladies. Not only was she from out of town, they weren't sure if she was really from the South. To a Northerner, this may sound peculiar. Arkansas is not New Jersey, but it isn't Alabama-Mississippi-Georgia-Tennessee either! So the shower lasted a little longer than normal.

Boys were not invited to showers. The women in the Circle always referred to the opposite gender as "boys," no matter their age. The "boys" sat in their trucks and cars in the church parking lot, waiting to drive home their wives, girlfriends, moms, or brides-to-be when the shower finally ended. And of course, shower-waiting had rituals as rich as shower-attending.

Grooms-to-be were allowed by the ladies of Circle #4 to come into the social room only at the very end of the shower to help load up all the loot. There was, however, an expectation that the male intruder give the appropriate oos and ahs when cued with a "Come look at this!" It was also the opportunity for one of the senior ladies to pull the groom-to-be aside and render the verdict from their bride-to-be inspection. Having talked with some of the "ol' boys" during the shower-waiting part, I had learned a bit about the ladies' special scoring system.

The highest score you could get was "You don't deserve her," usually pronounced after a stern "Boy!" and a very long pause. That designation, however, was typically reserved for a member of the high school homecoming court, whose family's family's family had helped charter the church. "Lovely" and "special" were sort of the next-best category. The barely passing grade was usually a plural pronouncement, like, "I know you two will be very happy." Miss Lena was the chosen pronouncer.

I was passing by the choir-rehearsal room in the church educational building on my way to the car with an armful when she almost timidly pulled me aside. The look on her face telegraphed her dilemma. This inspection was unique. My assertive, high-spirited, obviously very bright bride-to-be from out of town (and possibly out of the South) had defied their grading protocols.

"Be tolerant," she said. I was confused! Was this a grade the ol' boys had missed, a piece of advice, or a roundabout way of admitting: "We don't know how to grade what you have chosen, so go and be tolerant!"? Then, she added, "You'll do fine if you're just tolerant." Over the next 35 years, I learned that Miss Lena was "in the right church, but the wrong pew."

CUSTOMER LOVE NEEDS STRETCH, NOT SUFFERANCE

Miss Lena thought the best way to remain in a love relationship with a high spirited, mind-of-her-own partner was to be tolerant. But love relationships don't require tolerance. They require elasticity! And customer devotion is no different.

Tolerance implies a kind of stoic patience, an enduring res- ignation. It suggests the tone Mrs. Pope used in our fifth-grade class when she sighed her familiar and patronizing, "We'll all wait until Chip decides to settle down and join the rest of us." Tolerance conveys endurance and fortitude. That's not the cus- tomer-devotion way. Partnerships require give and flex; they expand to accommodate.

Tolerance-based relationships are exercises in sufferance. There is a degree of rigidity about them. Such rigid relation- ships have the volume turned up on every flaw and error. People in relationships based on tolerance are perpetually pained by partner imperfections, but silently suffer without comment. There is a type of resignation, as in, "This unfortu- nate disruption just 'comes with the territory.'"

Elasticity is about buoyancy, the opposite of rigidity. Elastic relationships have shock absorbers. They expand and unfold in their acceptance; little bumps in the rocky road of relationship are absorbed without attention. It is the difference between a telephone pole and a willow.

Jack Russell Rainey was the King of Rural Mail Route #1 in Northeast Arkansas. Jack's letter-carrier route was one he took over after his father retired from the U.S. Post Office. Now, if you were in the grocery store with Jack when he happened to encounter one of his "boxholders," as he called his customers, you would instantly spot a relationship based on two-way devo- tion. Jack was also my wife's father.

On one visit, I asked Aunt Rachel about Jack's secret to mail magic. I knew she had spent many years listening to the many spoken cheers from Jack's many fans. "He brags about their fudge," she said, as if I would instantly catch the meaning and knowingly respond, "Oh, I see." Instead, I responded with puz- zlement: "But Jack's allergic to chocolate."

"That's just the point," she said, pride resonating in her voice. "You see, Jack has a way of accepting his boxholders as they are, and adoring them as he finds them." Most folks might turn down an offer like "I just baked you some fresh brownies" with a "Thanks, but I trying to watch my weight." Jack not only graciously took whatever they offered (there were others at Jack's house who loved chocolate), he asked for their recipe.

Now, Jack wasn't just buttering up the lonely, blue-haired widows who had little to do but crochet and cook. It was Jack's orientation to all relationships. When Jack was asked, "Where's a good place to fish?", he'd reveal his secret fishing hole on Black River. Despite his severe allergies to cat hair, he enjoyed (not endured) a 40-year continuous string of adopted kittens.

CUSTOMER LOVE IS NURTURED THROUGH RESILIENCE MORE THAN ENDURANCE

Customer love is about affirming relationships more through ebb and flow than give and take. It is encouraging elbow room rather than close inspection. It is seeking ways to open rather than means to close. Instead of nitpicking details, service providers with customer love in mind work to roll with normal imperfections.

What does this imply for organizations in pursuit of customer love? Instead of recoiling at small glitches, try rolling with unexpected jabs with an expansive "don't sweat the small stuff" orientation. When customers put too much energy into little details, surprise them by joyfully yielding on their "too loud" demands. You may shock them and delight yourself!

Examine your business practices. Do you make customers go to the nth degree to get what they need? Are there barriers that make it difficult to get an unusual request fulfilled? Do service-delivery systems evoke necessary tolerance in your customers? Try calling someone in your unit. Disguise your voice and ask for something unique or out of the ordinary. Do your associates expand or recoil? Do they tell, or do they ask?

McGuffy's Restaurants, headquartered in Asheville, North Carolina, has a norm: "The answer is 'Yes'; what is the question?" This "we'll figure out a way to do whatever you need" is a signal that assertive acceptance is more virtuous than stoic tolerance. It lets employees show the customer optimistic fluidness, not self-sacrificing indulgence.

Miss Lena was the epitome of tolerance. She was truly a devoted, sweet, and gentle woman. I learned shortly after her death at age 101 that her life philosophy was about endurance and tolerance. Perhaps her awkward pronouncement of the Circle's verdict had more to pronounce about her needs than my upcoming relationship adventure. That's okay. She gave it her best shot, and her heart was definitely devoted to my welfare.

Nancy Marie Rainey Bell is still the high-spirited, restless race horse she was 35 years ago. Sharing a relationship with her has taught me that tolerance only belongs in relationships without spirit—put tolerance in vigorous relationships, and you have a recipe for iron-handed conflicts and energy wasted on minutia.

Partnership elasticity, on the other hand, stretches the relationship so it can breathe and expand. And partners who flow together, grow together.

P.S. Nancy Marie Rainey was a member of her hometown homecoming court. Her family's family's family did charter the First Baptist Church in her Arkansas home town, and I don't deserve her!

13

GENEROSITY: GIVING MORE THAN YOU EXPECT TO GET

Worth Williamson's dad was serious about picking names. He could have chosen to name his new son Edward or Thomas. Both were solid family names. But taking his inspiration from the great retailer, James Cash Penny, he passed on his own first name and the legacy that went with it—Worth Williamson, Jr. It was to be prophetic (or maybe it was just Pygmalian: less a sign of the future than a self-fulfilling prophesy).

Worth was for several years my banker while I lived in Charlotte, North Carolina. Worth was the founder, CEO, and visionary leader of the First Charlotte Bank. I was an early customer when there was only a single branch at the corner of Queens and Providence. Today, the bank is called Centura and has many branches, each with Worth's "namesake trademark"—*service with worth*.

When I heard the wise-cracking, gum-smacking center fielder played by Madonna in the film *A League of Their Own* say, "Mae's not a name, it's an attitude," I thought of Worth. The line says volumes about Worth's approach to partnering with customers. Worth is not just the tag he answers to; it's his attitude.

Worth founded the bank with customer love in mind. He wanted the kind of neighborly experience most customers would warmly recall from their past. Consequently, First Charlotte Bank was the only bank in town with an old-fashioned, help-yourself popcorn machine in the lobby. It was the only bank that, on rainy days, erected a canvas tunnel to connect the parking lot with the lobby. I think First Charlotte's automatic teller machines were the first in town to state, "Good morning, Dr. Bell" on the instruction screen when I inserted my bank card. While most front-line bank employees in the city dressed in costumes on Halloween, First Charlotte's employees followed that practice on a lot more days. There was a bunny at Easter; elves at Christmas.

Cartoons festooned the driver's side of drive-in windows. Drive-in tellers gave out doggy treats along with the receipts to patrons who had canines in their cars. The list goes on, but you get the idea. Worth gave his customers worth. And in turn, his customers thought he was worthy of their business—all of it.

Worth has an abundance attitude. His take on life is, "I have gifts to share with all who pass my way. The more I share, the more gifts I will have to share. The more gifts I share, the more people there will be with whom I can share."

THE HARVEST OF ABUNDANCE IS MUTUAL GROWTH

Worth-style service is about mutual growth—a circular process that acts like a snowball rolling downhill. Abundance-based customer service is not a zero-sum, formulaic proposition. Native Americans did it with corn—plant the best, and the crop will grow more bountiful each year. Worth "planted" his best in customers, and all grew as a result.

We live in an era of economic ambivalence. Contemporary buying, selling, and serving are about maintaining margins on one side and finding bargains on the other. Customers want it fast, cheap, and their way. They also want it "good." They are unwilling to sacrifice any one attribute for another. This makes the service equation particularly challenging as cost-cutting companies carve full-time employees from payrolls. Left over are fewer people to serve more customers, and a growing proportion of these employees are part-timers with potentially less commitment to fight for marketplace victories.

Against this backdrop, there is a clash in store when an abundance attitude steps on stage. "Where is the worth in giving when taking is so crucial to survival?" some may chide. "Besides, before we can talk bounty, we need to get past survival. And what can Worth teach us beyond fluffy fads, clever campaigns, and manners like our mothers taught us? Our stakeholders cannot spend good feelings or deposit thank-you notes in their checking accounts." Worth knows that demonstrating a devotion to the customer builds loyalty, which builds retention, which builds success.

A friend of ours, Stew Leonard, runs a large grocery store in New England. He tells of a time when a customer returned to the store after buying a 99-cent quart of egg nog. "It's spoiled!" she complained. Stew recounts, "I smelled her egg nog and realized it just smelled like egg nog. The date stamp was way in the future. The carton had been opened, and the egg nog could not be resold. I felt refunding her money was not the fiscally responsible action. Besides, I wanted to set an example of being frugal. When I refused to refund her money, the woman said she was never again coming back to my store."

"So," you may be saying at this point, "you win some, you lose some. That's just the nature of customer service." Stew continues toward his punch line. "That evening as I reflected on my late-in-the-day actions, I remembered that our average customer spends close to $100 in our store about 50 weeks a year. A loyal customer stays with us 10 years before moving elsewhere. My save-a-penny action had saved our store 99 cents, but it cost our store $50,000. I decided to stop being short-term smart and long-term stupid!"

GENEROSITY IS A FOCUS ON RELATIONSHIP VALUE, NOT ON TRANSACTION COSTS

The worth of great customer service requires a focus not on the transaction costs, but on the relationship value. Transaction costs are not irrelevant, but they can, if we aren't careful, become destructively dominant. Loyal customers spend more money each year they are with you. Devoted customers become an extension of your sales and marketing efforts; their word-of-mouth accolades bring others. They help you improve by providing feedback, not as a disappointed consumer, but as an ally. Loyal customers assertively demonstrate commitment to your success.

There *are* fickle customers on the prowl for a cheap "one night stand" they can brag about as a financial conquest. However, smart service providers seek more mature customer relationships with customers in whom they can invest for a long-term payback. Smart money is on retention and loyalty, not acquisition; the wise enterprise counts on depth and length of relationship, not a single transaction.

Worth Williamson was clever enough to discover that popcorn, cartoons, and costumes might bring you in, but it was devotion and love that would bring you back. He kept tabs on my business challenges and triumphs. "How did your seminar go in New York last week?" he would remember to ask. "That article you wrote on service recovery really helped me. I made copies for all my managers." While very skilled at unearthing customer aims, he was also adept at unleashing customer affirmations.

My car battery died one day in the First Charlotte Bank parking lot—a 48-month battery in its 64th month! The nearest Wal-Mart/Sears/Firestone was two miles away. I went into the bank to call for transportation to a store to buy a replacement. "Take my car," Worth said as he overheard my call in the lobby. I turned to see the keys to his station wagon dangling from his extended hand. His gesture went way beyond the "use the phone in my office if you like" type offers. Worth is a devotee of expressions of plenty, not acts of politeness.

An abundance attitude has magnetic impact on customers. It attracts them because it conveys to the customer the kind of unconditional positive regard that characterizes relationships at their best. Customers like the way they feel when dealing with service providers who have such an orientation. They feel valued, not used. They enjoy relationships laced with substance and value far more than encounters that are functional, but hollow.

The noncompetitive nature of customer love means approaching the relationship with a "cast bread upon the water" orientation. And each contribution to the relationship causes it to grow and prosper. An abundance attitude creates a legacy of affirmation—it lives on in the language customers use to describe the service provider.

14

THE LEADER OF A CUSTOMER-LOVE CULTURE

I went to *Roget's Thesaurus* for inspiration. I hadn't really looked at *Roget's* since I was trying to write a term paper for Mrs. Ridley's 12th-grade English composition class. "What message would I get," I wondered, "if I looked up 'service' and thought about leadership?" I was surprised at how much I learned.

The word "service" has many meanings. It might mean *assistance or help*, as in, "We are here to be of service." But the word can also mean *duty*, as in, "Were you in the service?" It can also imply *ceremony*, as in, "We went to the 11 o'clock service." And finally, it can suggest *maintenance*, as in, "I took my car in for its 10,000-mile service." (I skipped over references to amorous bulls, servitude, and silver eating utensils.) But these four meanings—assistance, duty, ceremony and maintenance—suggest a role description of the service leader in a customer-love culture.

ASSISTANCE: THE LEADER AS HELPER

Service leadership in the past meant control and consistency. The "boss" of yesteryear kept a tight rein, otherwise employees would get lazy and fail to work. We now know that employees act like adults when they are treated like adults. And customer love depends on associates acting as adults. Employees who manage a tight family budget, buy and sell real estate, prepare complex tax returns, and juggle dentist appointments with soccer games and ballet lessons probably have the wisdom and maturity to handle almost any work assignment. No one at home ensures they have empowerment or "appropriate supervision." No one at home completes their annual performance appraisal to ensure they get "an accurate assessment of their efforts and deficiencies." Yet they manage the roles of parent and spouse and citizen just fine.

The service leader's role is to support and serve employees. That means running interference and getting employees the resources they need for effective work. It means planning, blazing new trails, and creating ways to be more effective as a team. It means treating employees as a very important customer segment and finding ways to meet their needs.

But who's in charge of control and consistency? As service leader, you still are! However, it is now something you pursue *with* employees, not something you *impose on* them. If employees are clear on organization and team goals, if they know the reasons "why," and if they know the real (and relevant) boundaries, they will *help* you ensure control and consistency, if allowed. Look for ways to involve, include, and invite.

DUTY: THE LEADER AS ROLE MODEL

When I was a new infantry officer, about to assume my first combat assignment in Vietnam, I asked the first sergeant what he thought my most important job was if I wanted to be a good officer. He didn't hesitate. "Be a good soldier," he said. It was his way of saying I needed to make sure my actions were always consistent with what I was asking the troops to be and do. It is the leader's first duty to honor a set of values through congruent actions.

Employees watch your moves, not your mouth. Cowboy humorist Will Rogers said it better: "People learn more from *observation* than from *conversation*." If you are telling employees that service is really important, then are you personally demonstrating that priority through what you do? Effective leaders learn to be clear about their values and seek every day to live professional lives that are consistent with those values, especially in moments of tough choices. If your employees watched where you put your energy for one week, what would they conclude is your top priority? Is that priority the legacy you would hope to leave your organization?

CEREMONY: THE LEADER AS CHEERLEADER

A few years ago, one of my partners and I consulted with a successful insurance company, whose average, non-supervisory, professional employee was 27 years old and earned about $85,000 a year. Most were highly driven, Ivy League college-educated go-getters. Yet, an employee-attitude survey revealed that they regarded themselves as under-rewarded. We first thought we were dealing with a bunch of spoiled brats who had no idea how the real world worked or that only a tiny fraction of the world's population made that kind of money. But we were wrong. "We know we are very well compensated," they told me. "We just do not feel valued and recognized for what we do." They were living examples of psychologist William James' observation: "The deepest principle of human nature is the craving to be appreciated."

Effective service leaders celebrate. This does not mean the perfunctory retirement dinner or perfect-attendance ceremony. These are fine, but they are not enough. Great leaders look for occasions to publicly affirm excellence. They look for opportunities to tell stories of what they want others to model and emulate. They know they get more of what they recognize.

MAINTENANCE: THE LEADER AS TUTOR

Great service leaders know that quality improvement is continuous and that learning is never over. They know that if they want a climate of creativity and growth, they must honor learning and teaching. "He not busy being born is busy dying," Bob Dylan wrote in one of his early folk songs. It is also true of organizations. As the world of service quality continues to change and get more complex, it is crucial that the service leader act as a mentor—always helping others learn and improve. Just as machines need proper maintenance to go the distance, so do people. In the organizational world, people maintenance involves increased competence and wisdom.

What does great service leadership entail? It means remembering that employees are your most important customers. They will give customers the quality of service they receive from their leaders. It means always ensuring that your actions are in sync with the actions employees observe. The values you live are the values they believe you honor. It means finding ways to inspire by making work inspirational. And it means helping employees learn, especially when they make errors.

The decade ahead will require even more focus on the customer than the past decade. The winning organizations will be those with great leaders, not efficient administrators. Successful leaders will be those willing to turn the organizational pyramid upside down and daily work to serve those who serve the customer. Be a responsive helper in your assistance role, a valued role model in your duty role, an inspirational cheerleader in your ceremony role, and a caring mentor in your maintenance role.

15

THE LOVE LEADER
AS LISTENER

I bet there are not more than two supervisors on the face of the globe who do not know the importance of being a good listener. It matters not whether the person ever attended a leadership class, read an article on supervision, or witnessed a manager who was a good listener. Turn on the tube, pick up a newspaper, or just hang out in the bar, and the virtues of listening will come creeping through. If you've never heard of the importance of listening, you're a card-carrying alien from some other galaxy.

Knowing that listening is important and *being* a good listener are two very different things. Ask employees about the listening skills of their bosses, and most will give bosses at best a C+! Why is it that, with zillions of books on how leaders should listen, employees continue to ding their bosses on listening? Is this a competence crisis? I think the gap between "should" and "would" has less to with communication management and more to do with noise management.

Most leaders *can* be great listeners. Let their eight-year-old come crying about a neighborhood conflict, and you will see great listening. Zero in on a quiet, corner conversation in the funeral home during the wake of a friend, and you will see great listening. Put a leader between a hostile union steward and potential shut-you-down strike, and you will witness some of the best listening in history. Yet, mix the normal pace of work, the typical persona of "I'm the boss," and the traditional orientation that "employees don't need to be babied," and you have the prescription for "just get to the punch line" listening.

Listening is crucial to creating and sustaining a culture famous for customer love. Yet, we have a paradox. Leaders *can* be great listeners. And employees who experience great leader-listening report it as magical. Yet, employees say their bosses are generally C+ listeners. How do leaders translate an A+ potential into an A+ performance? How do leaders dodge the dogged demands of daily distractions to deliver dedicated listening? The sounds of great listening tell us effective listeners don't *start* doing anything special, they *stop* doing something normal.

FOCUS ON FOCUS

Love leaders get focused and stay focused. When listening is their goal, they make it *the* priority. They do not let *anything* distract. A wise leader said, "There are no individuals at work more important to your success than your employees—not your boss, not your customers, not your vendors. When an employee needs you to listen, pretend you just got a gift of five minutes with your greatest hero; for me it is Abraham Lincoln." What a great concept! Think about it. If you could have five minutes, and *only* five minutes, with Moses, Mozart, or Mother Teresa, would you let a call from your boss, your customer, or *anyone* eat up part of that precious time? Treat your employees with the same focus and priority.

"Hold my calls," "Let's get out of here so we can really talk," or "Tell him I'll have to call back" are words that telegraph noise management. They say to employees, "What you have to say is so important, I do not want to miss one word." If you cannot give employees that "I've got five minutes with Kissenger" kind of focus, postpone the encounter until you can. It is better to say: "Jane, I want to give you my undivided attention. But I'm two hours from a crucial meeting, and I would honestly only be giving you half of my attention. Can we schedule this later today when I can really focus?"

ASSUME THE REPORTER POSITION

Try something next time you need to listen to someone. Assume you are a newspaper reporter from another planet sent here on assignment to "get the story" and report it. Your readers cannot "see," "hear," or "feel" this story except through your words. And they are also handicapped by not really understanding this culture. So, you must rely on every tiny clue, nuance, or symbol to get the story right.

Your first interviewee is right now sitting before you talking. It is your employee. Now, staying in the stance of an alien reporter, consider every subtlety in her or his tone, gesture, or expression. Notice the eyes—what some have labeled "the window to the soul." Pretend you do not know this person and you are hearing him or her speak to you for the first time. Listen for choice of words and expressions. Is there a deeper meaning behind the sentences you hear? Is there a message that is not initially obvious in the communication?

If you ask a question or make a statement, how quick is his or her answer or response? What might be implied by silence? Is her or his laughter polite, muted, or hearty? Wonder why? If his words and tone could be a song, what style of music would it be? Is it a country song, a rap tune, a chorale, or a gospel hymn? If a great painter used this person's words as the inspiration for a picture, what might you end up seeing appear on the canvas?

Listening done well is complete absorption. Have you ever watched Larry King on CNN? His success as a superb interviewer lies not in his questions, but in his terrific listening skills. He zips right past the interviewees words, sentences, and paragraphs to get to the interviewee's message, intent, and meaning. The mission of listening is to be so crystal clear on the other person's message that it becomes "copy and paste" execution command from one brain's computer screen to another's. Perhaps the expression "meeting of the minds" should be changed to "joining of the minds." Dramatic listening goes beyond a mere rendezvous of brains. It is more a uniting, a linkage, a partnership. And like all human connections, there is a requirement for constant effort and obvious commitment.

BE A MIRROR, NOT A MEMORY

One of my biggest challenges in my striving to be a good parent was to simply listen without an agenda. As my son began to catalog his concerns, convictions, or curiosity, I would usually feel the need to make a point, teach a lesson, correct an action, or offer some caution. When I finally gave up trying to be a smart daddy and worked at being a simple mirror, he began to open up, trust, and most important, feel heard. I still have to work at being a caring mirror rather than a wise memory.

When he would ask, "How would you ...?", I worked hard to remember to have him tell me what he would do before offering my opinions. When he voiced a frustration or concern, I tried to first communicate to him through my actions that his message got through before I delivered an answer, especially when my answer was likely to be different than the one he thought he was going to get.

PUT YOUR ASSOCIATES IN CHARGE OF CUEING YOU

Being a poor listener is habit forming. Focusing takes effort; mirroring takes patience. Meanwhile, the clock is ticking on getting that order out, and the boss is wanting to know where the late McAllister report is you promised. There are two calls holding, three people in the waiting room, and you're finishing up a meeting with an employee. Who could be a great listener under these circumstances? Answer: Not even Superman! You need assistance from the *only* person who can assist you—your employee.

Help comes in the following form: "George, I need your help. I know there are times when I'm not the listener I want to be. But most of the time, when I'm being a lousy listener, I'm not aware I'm doing it. That's where you can help. When you think you are *not* getting my undivided attention, I'd appreciate your letting me know. I may get better, I may reschedule our meeting to a better time, or I may just keep on being a lousy listener. But I don't have a shot at improving unless I know I need to, and you are the best person to tell me."

People are not stupid! They hear the words of your request, but will be skeptical until they witness consistent actions. Your request for employee feedback on your listening will take being repeated several times before people are likely to believe you enough to try it. And the first three or four times employees actually offer you feedback, they'll need to hear you express your sincere gratitude, regardless of how well it went or how accurate their suggestion might be. Prime the feedback pump, dramatically listen to (and value) whatever you get, and in time the quality and helpfulness of the feedback will improve.

Love leaders do not listen—a passive activity; they listen *dramatically*. They demonstrate through their words and actions that the words of their employees are valued and important. When people feel heard, they feel valued. Feeling valued, they are more likely to take risks and experiment. Only through trying new steps do they grow and learn. The bottom line is this: If your goal is to be a great leader, start by using your noise management skills to help you fully use your talents as a great listener.

16

THE LOVE LEADER AS
TRUST GIVER

The most famous car in Charlotte, North Carolina, in 1971 was a perfectly restored, antique Mercedes Benz sports car owned and driven daily by Luther Hodges, Jr. Luther was then chairman of the board of North Carolina National Bank and the son of a former North Carolina governor and cabinet member under President John Kennedy. Tall, handsome, and Harvard educated, Luther was an impressive leader. Coupled with the car, he was just plain impressive.

I had been with the bank only a few months and considered myself to be about 347 levels below Luther. My occasional meetings with him were always cordial, warm, and upbeat. He went out of his way to help soothe my too obvious nervousness at being in the presence of "the chairman." I wanted to learn from him, and he clearly afforded me the opportunity. However, the emotional space between us felt too wide for me—certainly not for him. I picked my words carefully in his presence. Learning from Mr. Hodges always took a back seat to impressing Mr. Hodges. Until the car changed everything.

Luther, my boss, and I were meeting in Raleigh, about three hours from Charlotte, the city where we all lived and worked. My boss and I had driven there in the company Ford. Luther had driven there in his Mercedes. Our meeting went late, and Luther and my boss decided to stay over another night and drive back together early the next morning so they could talk on the drive.

Two small problems remained: How was I going to get back to Charlotte that evening, and how was the Mercedes going to get back to Charlotte? (The Ford was checked out in my boss's name, and only he could drive it.)

"Chip, why don't you take my car home with you," said Luther, flashing his Steinway smile. "Drive into work in the morning, park in my spot, and just leave the keys with Pam. I'll give you a ride home tomorrow afternoon." I remember my ears ringing, my heart pounding, and my being unable to speak for what seemed like an eternity. The chairman wanted me to drive his car to my home! Curtains of distance fell to the floor. This "god-like creature" was transformed instantly into my wise friend. He trusted me with his most prized possession. My anxiety was converted into confidence.

Love leadership will only work with trust. While trust comes from experience, the origin of trust is risk. And when leaders trust associates, associates reciprocate in kind. Trust is powerful in all relationships. It makes marriages, friendships, and all manner of alliances work, and work well. However, trust has a special power in relationships in which there is, by definition, unequal power. Trust is the equalizer.

PUT YOUR ASSOCIATE "ON THE RIGHT"

At an early age, I learned through school and church that "sitting on the right" was a special privilege. Kings put their most important ally on their right when attending a banquet. The Bible makes many references to "sitting on the right hand of God." Years later, I learned the origin of the concept. Most kings (and writers of scripture) were right-handed. In the era of sword and dagger, the right side was the least defensible to a right handed person. To unsheathe a sword with the right hand and then strike to the close right was extremely awkward. So, the person most trusted was invited to join the most vulnerable position. It became a station of honor.

The counterpart to "putting the associate on your right" is doing some action that deliberately, as well as symbolically, communicates trust and honor. Luther let me drive home his car. As someone now past age 50, I am a bit embarrassed at the impact such an action had on me. From today's perspective, my reaction back then feels rather juvenile and immature. But if I roll my life camera back 25 years and reflect on the experience, I remember it as dramatic and impactful.

The most effective "sitting on the right" actions are those unique to the individual. They dramatically demonstrate two aspects of the relationship: a deep understanding of the individual and a recognition that trust is created through trustful (full of trust) actions. A friend of mine recalls a time when his boss sent him to a very important meeting in his place. One of my partners describes a time in which a giant in his field was unable to keep an engagement and recommended my partner to be his replacement. I once had a boss who, because of an unexpected call to go out of the country, asked me to interview a candidate for a very senior position in the company, and said I was welcome to use his executive suite office to conduct the interview. While I elected to interview the candidate in my own plain vanilla office far from mahogany row, his gesture communicated a special trust.

Demonstrate Humility "Squared"

One of the most trusted organizations in the world today is Johnson & Johnson. Their reputation was elevated during their darkest hour—the Tylenol incident. Instead of covering up and making excuses, the company spent over $100 million to remove every Tylenol container from shelves around the world and went overboard in wall-to-wall honesty and openness. Actor Hugh Grant's reputation suffered only a slight blip on the screen with his escapade with a prostitute because he stood up to the challenge, acknowledged his "sins," and asked for the public's forgiveness. Dee Dee Myers, former press secretary to

President Clinton, received similar reaction by demonstrating public humility after being stopped by police for driving while legally intoxicated.

All relationships have hiccups and less-than-perfect moments. The leader who steps up to the plate and dramatically demonstrates humility and authenticity is the leader who nurtures trust. Luther not only loaned me his car, he was also able to level with me about his own errors, struggles, and challenges. The more I witnessed his humility, the more he was trustworthy.

At a large social event in Ovens Auditorium in Charlotte, North Carolina, Luther formally announced his candidacy for the U.S. Senate with a speech. Drawing heavily from obvious note cards, the audience politely listened to his awkward speech. (Luther was never very comfortable as a public speaker.) Halfway through the speech, he lost his place because his cards were out of order. He cracked an apologetic comment and ad-libbed for a moment as he struggled to find his place. Before he could fully recover, the large audience broke into supportive applause. It was the sincere, genuine Luther they adored, not Luther with notes. Mask removal is the humble stuff of which trust is made.

Humility does not mean publicly falling on one's sword. It also does not imply loudly advertising warts and clay feet. It does mean working very hard to be vulnerable and open with protégés. It means remaining alert for opportunities to show empathy "I know how you feel" rather than sympathy "I feel how you feel." It entails working to strip any nuance of rank, power, or status from the relationship. Great relationships need to be egalitarian, not laced with sovereignty.

CAREFULLY COMMUNICATING COMPETENCE

Larry N. Davis of Austin and Dr. Duane Tway of Tucson have broken new ground in the field of interpersonal trust. "Trust," according to Davis and Tway, "is defined as a state of readiness for unguarded interaction with some one or thing."

We lower our human shields, they posit, only if the perceived intention of the other person is pure, and if their perceived competence is valued. In other words, we trust those people whom we: 1) believe are not out to do us in, and 2) perceive have the capacity to do what we trust them to do. We do not trust leaders to be great leaders if we believe they have little to help us learn.

The challenge is one of communicating eligibility without displaying arrogance. How does the leader show smartness without being a smart aleck? While humility is always a virtue, too much humbleness can threaten follower confidence in the leader. Self-effacing comments, while initially a symbol of modesty, can erode faith if carried too far. "Great leaders," said Luther to one of my advanced leadership classes, "are willing to let followers see their weak sides. And they are willing to let followers see their strong sides." Call it wholeness, balance, or congruence, the goal is a displayed persona that engenders trust.

Let the employee hear your pride in your ability. Pride communicates acknowledged good fortune, not boastfulness. Be quick to credit others with your abilities, if possible. "I was really lucky to be the understudy for Tom Connellan. One of the things Tom taught me was . . . " Send a tone that whatever competence you possess is competence you are anxious to share with the follower. Show your enthusiasm for transmitting your abilities to the follower. Arrogance is less about what one has and more about what one attempts to hoard. The goal is to let the employee know you hold something of superior value, but that holding it does not make you superior.

Putting the "us" in trust involves remembering that trust is an interpersonal dimension. Trust is something that happens within people only when it is created between people. However, trust is not something that happens by accident; trust is crafted "by hand." It takes personalized action and attention to the impact which actions have on associates.

And where does that leave us with Luther and *the car*? Luther unfortunately lost in his primary bid for a U.S. Senate seat, but went on to become undersecretary of commerce under President Carter, followed by a stint as chairman of the board of a Washington, D.C. bank. He currently manages a variety of entrepreneurial ventures in Phoenix. He kept the Mercedes for many years, finally selling it while in D.C. After 30 years, we still correspond. And there are very few people in the world I would trust more than Chairman Hodges.

17

THE LOVE LEADER
AS EMPOWERER

Empowerment. The word is spoken with apprehension by most managers. What races through their heads are scary images of "employees giving away the store" and "bosses giving up control." Some employees want more of it; some want to be told what to do and not worry about work after five o'clock.

Every time I hear someone exhorting managers to "empower" their employees, I remember Joseph B. O'Shea, the boss of my first full-time job out of school. Joe was a crusty ex-union buster who had started out in the textile mills of South Carolina, kicking butts and taking names, as he liked to say. Many fellow employees lost their breakfast worrying about an upcoming meeting with Mr. O'Shea.

One day Joe called a meeting to announce that the company was shifting to a participative management philosophy. The idea of Joe being participative was about as likely as Attila the Hun being compassionate. But Joe was a very good soldier. If the company wanted people to be more participative, he'd give it his best shot. However, we were reassured that the world as we knew it was not about to come crashing down when Joe ended the meeting with: "Our division *will* have participative management. And you'll participate, or I'll fire your a_ _!"

Joe's heart was in the right place, but he completely missed the point. As managers struggle with "close encounters of the empowerment kind," there is potential to fall into a similar trap.

121

Like Joe, most managers want to do the right thing. And like Joe, some risk missing the point.

WHY IS EMPOWERMENT IMPORTANT?

The world of business is changing—for customers, for managers, for employees. For customers, the standards of what counts as great service are climbing. Why? Because customers evaluate product quality differently from the way they evaluate service quality. Customers wanting to buy a computer only compare it to other computers. They don't compare a new computer with a new washing machine or fishing rod. But service is different. Customers compare the service from any organization with *anybody* giving great customer service—Disney, FedEx, Nordstrom, you name it. That dramatically raises the bar on the standards for customer service.

One element of this rising service standard is having employees with the authority to make a decision on behalf of the customer. The customer who just had a department store clerk make a quick exception to the return policy or had a waiter "comp" the dessert because of slow service, is not thrilled to then hear any employee anywhere timidly say, "I'll have to check with my manager," or curtly say, "That's our policy." Customers want an experience without hassle or delay.

The relationship between a boss and subordinate is also changing. The old view of manager as "company parent" has been altered to that of manager as supporter, coach, even partner. And as employees demonstrate the maturity to work effectively with limited supervision, empowerment becomes a necessity. Most employees manage the complexities of their home lives very well. They're not enthused about then coming to work and having to check their brains at the time clock. So, what do empowering managers do?

What is Empowerment?

Empowerment is ensuring that employees closest to a problem or need have the authority to make judgments on how the problem is solved or how the need is met. Empowerment does not mean unlimited license—"Just do whatever you need to do." It means responsible freedom. It means helping employees balance the freedom to go the extra mile for the customer with the responsibility of taking care of the organization. Bottom line, it's helping employees have the perspective of an owner.

Empowerment is not a gift given to employees by managers. When managers ask, "How do I empower my employees?" you get a sense they're thinking of it as a gift. The job of the manager is to release power—to remove barriers that keep employees from acting with power.

How does Empowerment Work?

Empowerment works when managers examine the work environment and their own practices to identify barriers to responsible freedom. Below are four common barriers, along with a few tips on how to eliminate each barrier.

1. No Purpose. Today's employees work smarter when they feel a part of an important mission. And they make more responsible decisions on behalf of the organization and the customer. When asked, "What are you doing?", the apathetic bricklayer stated the obvious, "Laying bricks." But the committed bricklayer answered, "I'm building a great cathedral." Purpose or mission provides employees a focus on the cathedral-building mission, not just the brick-laying task.

FedEx chairman Fred Smith reminds FedEx employees of their purpose or mission: "You aren't just delivering stuff by 10:30 a.m. You transport the most precious cargo in the world—an organ for a vital transplant, a gift for a special ceremony, a factory part that may halt the work of a company."

There's no better illustration of how purpose permeates FedEx than the company's role in the rescue of Jessica McClure, the little Texas girl who became trapped in a well several years ago. Specialized drilling equipment was needed to sink a shaft beside the trapped girl to rescue her. The FedEx agent who received the late-night request to transport the equipment immediately dispatched a standby FedEx jet. At that moment, that drill was the most precious cargo in the world. Her priority was to see it delivered ASAP, not to hide behind the barrier of determining who would foot the bill. No one at FedEx views that as out of the ordinary.

What you can do. Talk about your mission often. Focus on what you want the unit, team, or organization to *be*, not just what you want it to *do*. Communicate the "whys" when making assignments, not just the "whats" and "whens." Recognize heroes by telling their stories—especially the details of their accomplishments that are examples of the mission.

Walk the talk. Make sure your actions are consistent with your mission or purpose. Where do you spend time? What do you show excitement or worry about?

2. No Protection. Empowerment begins with error. Employees learn quickly whether they're empowered when they make a mistake. If the error is met with rebuke, it sends a very different message than if managers see error as an opportunity for learning and problem solving. Isn't it unlikely that the person in charge of hiring employees said, "Let me see how many dumb, malicious, or shiftless employees I can hire this week"? Yet, notice how quickly an error-making employee can be labeled as stupid, evil, or lazy, and on whose watch?

Without risk, there's no learning, no creativity, and no motivation. With risk, there are occasional, honest mistakes. It's easier to gently rein in an over-zealous, go-the-extra-mile employee than to find one with an enthusiastic attitude in the first place. Empowering is trusting. The greater the trust, the greater the freedom. But freedom comes with responsibility. The manager's job is to coach employees to feel more comfortable with more responsibility.

What you can do. Examine procedures. Employees may feel unprotected due to past practice. Are employees clear on what is a "thou shalt not" law versus what is an "it would be better if you didn't" guideline? Recall a time when an employee made an honest mistake. Was forgiveness spoken, or just implied? Are employees publicly given the benefit of the doubt? Do they get more coaching, or more critiquing? How many times do employees get praised for excellent efforts that failed to work? Are employees commended for seeking assistance from others, including other managers?

3. No Permission. Employees need guidelines, not unlimited license. The manager who says, "Just go do whatever you think is best," is probably demonstrating abdication, not empowerment. But guidelines need elbow room for the employee to adapt to the situation and customer. Customers don't want uniformity in service. While they want consistency, they also want to be treated uniquely. This requires front-line flexibility.

It's dangerous to assume that employees will just know what they are and are not allowed to do—or even that they'll believe you the first time you say, "Yes, you can." Employees have probably been hearing "no" for a long time. Empowerment takes some getting used to—for managers and employees.

What you can do. Examine your reward and recognition practices. Which is more valued: creativity or compliance? Being resourceful or being always right? Who gets praised or promoted—and for what? Apply the "zero-based" budgeting concept to rules. If you eliminated *all* the rules and polices, and then added back only those absolutely relevant, would you be writing restrictions long into the night?

4. No Proficiency. "Knowledge is power," said philosopher Francis Bacon. The capacity to find clever, resourceful, and creative solutions is the mark of a wise person prepared and empowered to go beyond the traditional and the ordinary. Training your employees, not once, but constantly, provides wisdom, not just competence. And whereas competence promotes confidence, wisdom fosters power.

Building competence also means sharing information about the organization. If you want employees to focus on long-term relationships with customers (and not be completely preoccupied with the transaction cost of each encounter) they need big-picture direction and details about the balance sheet. If you want employees to make front-line decisions like owners, they need the benefit of "owner-type information."

Empowerment is earned through knowledge. Early on, there's frustration as employees want to start "running things" and "don't know what they don't know." The manager has to take the time to "grow" employees. This takes openness, so both parties can ask questions, discuss issues, and share thoughts. Unless it's a crisis, the employee needs the chance to work through issues and learn from experience.

What you can do. Emphasize proficiency by recognizing employees whose performance stands out. Use them as mentors of others. Allow time in meetings for employees to share key learnings. Be a lifelong learner yourself. Your example is one employees will follow. Build a folklore of empowerment stories that communicate empowered actions that should be taken, and examples of how these are done.

What Are the Cautions?

Empowerment is a never-ending journey. Often, managers feel impatient with how long it takes. There is a great temptation to revert back to telling employees what to do and how to do it. Don't give in to this temptation. As employees learn the business, managers will feel more comfortable entrusting them with decisions and letting go. Customers will be more satisfied, employees will become more well-rounded, managers will be more able to focus on bigger-picture issues, and the journey will become a worthwhile trip.

Employees also have their challenges with empowerment. Overzealous front-line employees can make decisions without the experience or competence to do so. Again, it requires patience from both managers and employees. On the flip side, some employees may not grab the brass "E" ring as rapidly as managers would like. It can seem a lot safer to just "do what you're told," especially if the employee has been burned in the past for initiative that didn't pan out. Employees need to learn through experience that mistakes are tools for growth, not traps for punishment.

As long as organizations have people at different levels, empowerment will be a challenge. The wise leader recognizes the enormous power that can be harnessed when barriers to responsible freedom are eliminated and employees are encouraged to think like owners. Morale climbs, burnout is reduced, managers feel shared responsibility, and profits soar as customers rave about an organization full of value, joy, and power.

18
THE LOVE LEADER AS MENTOR

My mother-in-law had a five-and-dime-store parakeet named Pretty Boy. Over the years, she taught Pretty Boy to sing a bunch of songs. One day, she ordered a new vacuum cleaner. It came with a tube-shaped attachment she thought was perfectly suited to vacuum out Pretty Boy's birdcage. You know where this is going! The phone rang one day, and Pretty Boy ended up in the vacuum cleaner bag!

She panicked. Tearing open the vacuum bag, she found the parakeet alive, but totally covered with dust, dirt, and soot. She rushed the bird to the bath tub and turned on both tub faucets, almost drowning Pretty Boy. Realizing the error of her solution, she grabbed the hair dryer to blow dry the poor bird!

A few days later at the church social, the editor of the local newspaper heard of her catastrophe and sent a reporter around to get this unique, human-interest story. As the reporter was about to leave at the end of his interview, he asked my mother-in-law, "By the way, how's Pretty Boy now?"

Without expression or hesitation, she answered: "Pretty Boy doesn't sing anymore. He just sort of sits and stares."

We live in times of turbulent change. Far too many employees hired to "sing a bunch of songs" are traumatized almost daily by downsizing, reorganization, mergers, and just plain uncertainty. Some end up like Pretty Boy, "sitting and staring." Customers experience traumatized employees through rigid,

"Rules 'R' Us," front-line behavior. Managers witness "sitting and staring" when they observe compliance instead of commitment, inflexibility rather than creativity, and resistance instead of responsibility.

There is one group of employees, however, who "sing" in the midst of turmoil. Thriving on discord, this group turns dissonance into harmony. They are the learners in the organization. Learners are not only happier employees, but they are less likely to jump ship at the first sign of rough seas.

Expanding the number of "singers" is not likely to come by reducing the chaos; massive change is here to stay. Nor does it come by adding more training programs or expanding the tuition-refund policy. It entails altering the role of the leader from *corporate parent* to *compassionate partner*. It involves having all leaders add "learning coach" or "mentor" to their repertoire of roles.

THE MAGIC OF MENTORING

Mentor—the word conjures up an image of a seasoned, corporate sage conversing with a naive, still "wet behind the ears," young recruit. The conversation would likely be laced with informal rules, closely guarded secrets, and "I remember back when . . . " stories of daredevil heroics and too-close-to-call tactics. Mentoring has had an almost heady, academic sound, solely reserved for workers in white collars whose fathers advised, "Go get to know 'ol Charlie."

Mentoring in recent times is a label wrapped less around privilege and more around affirmative action. The minorities—whomever they may have been—got a mentor assigned to expedite their route through glass ceilings, beyond "old boys' networks," and past the private winks formerly reserved only for WASP males. Mentors of this type sometimes salved the consciences of those who could bravely "talk goodness," but who were squeamish if expected to spearhead courageous acts.

Mentoring programs sounded contemporary and forward-thinking. Some were of great service; many were lip service.

But what is mentoring, really? When the package is unwrapped and the political correctness is scraped away, what's left? A mentor is simply someone who helps someone else learn something he or she would have learned less well, more slowly, or not at all if left alone. Notice the power-free nature of this definition. Mentors are not power figures. Mentors are learning coaches—sensitive, trusted advisers.

The traditional use of the word "mentor" connotes a person outside one's usual chain of command who "helps me understand this crazy organization." Not all mentors are supervisors or managers. But all—I repeat *all*—supervisors and managers should be mentors. Mentoring must become simply that part of every leader's role that has growth as its primary outcome.

Organizations cannot afford to rely on mentoring programs for system-wide "singing." While mentoring programs can be helpful, they are simply inadequate in creating a learning organization. Every leader must mentor, and, he or she must mentor most those associates whose performance they influence, because in the words of consultant Arie De Geus, "Your ability to learn faster than your competition is your only sustainable competitive advantage."

CREATING A PARTNERSHIP FOR LEARNING

Mentoring employees is not easy. How do you carry out an "insight goal" from an "in charge" role? How does a supervisor or manager encourage a subordinate to experiment, make mistakes, and try new behaviors—all important to learning—from a "By the way, I'll be doing your performance review" position? Overcoming this authority obstacle to learning can only happen through a partnership relationship.

Mentoring from a partnership perspective is different from the classical "I'm the guru; you're the greenhorn" orientation. Mentoring from a partnership perspective means, "We are fel-

low travelers on this journey toward wisdom." Stated differently, the greatest gift a mentor can give his or her protégé is to
position that protégé as his or her mentor. However, a learning
partnership does not just happen, it must be created. And, the
mentor must take the lead in crafting it.

The main event of mentoring entails giving learning gifts—
advice, feedback, focus, and support. However, such learning
gifts may not readily be seen by the protégé as a desired present. Gifts, no matter how generously bestowed, may not always
be experienced with glee. Recall the last time someone said to
you, "Let me give you some advice," or "I need to give you a little feedback." You probably did more resisting than rejoicing.
Protégés are no different.

Smart mentors create a readiness for the main event of
mentoring. Protégés are more likely to experience the benevo-
lence of gifts if they are delivered in a relationship of safety,
advocacy, and equality.

FOUR STAGES OF MENTORING

Mentoring from a partnership perspective entails four stages:
1) leveling the learning field, 2) fostering acceptance and safety,
3) giving learning gifts, and 4) bolstering self-direction and
independence. The first two stages are aimed at creating a readiness for the main event—gifting. The final stage is about weaning the protégé from any dependence on the mentor.

Stage 1: Leveling the learning field. The first challenge a
mentor faces is to help the protégé experience the relationship as
a true partnership. Leveling the learning field means stripping the
relationship of any nuances of mentor power and command. It
entails surrendering to the process of learning rather than controlling or driving it. It requires creating rapport or kinship and
removing the mask of supremacy.

The word "rapport" is a French derivation which literally
means "a bringing back" or "connection renewed." The success of
a mentoring relationship can hang on early mentor-protégé

encounters; good starts foster good growth. The tone created in the first meeting can decide if the relationship will be fruitful or fraught with fear and anxiety. Quality learning will not occur until the shield has been lowered enough for the learner to take risks in front of the mentor. Rapport building expedites shield lowering.

The old Southern customs of bringing a gift when visiting a friend, bringing flowers on the first date, starting a speech with a joke, or engaging in small talk at the beginning of a sales call all signal that openings are rocky *and* important. What does rapport-building look like for a mentor?

Rapport begins with the sounds and sights of openness and authenticity. Any normal person approaching a potentially anxious encounter will raise her or his antennae high in search of early warnings regarding the road ahead. Will this situation embarrass me? Will this person take advantage of me? Will I be able to be effective with this encounter? Is there harm awaiting me?

Given this signal searching by the protégé, it is crucial for the mentor to be quick in transmitting a welcoming tone and feel. Open posture (e.g., no crossed arms), warm and enthusiastic reception, eye contact, removal of physical barriers, and personalized greetings are all gestures communicating an attempt to cultivate a level playing field. Mentors who rely on the artifacts of power (peering over an imposing desk, making the protégé do all the approaching, tight and closed body language, a reserved manner, or facial expressions that communicate distance) make grave errors in crafting the early ease important to relationship building.

Mentors often use a gifting gesture to signal a level learning field. The perfunctory "How about a cup of coffee?" is certainly a well-worn gifting gesture. However, think about how much more powerful a statement like, "I had my assistant locate this article; I thought you might find it useful" could be as early evidence that this relationship will be a power-free one. I once had a mentor who kept a supply of his wife's homemade jellies for visitors, and the gift was always bestowed very early in the encounter, not at the end. Strip any nuance of sovereignty from the relationship, and focus on crafting a learning partnership.

Stage 2: Fostering acceptance and safety. Great mentors who are effective at fostering acceptance avoid testing tones, judgmental gestures, and parental positions. Great mentors show acceptance through focused and dramatic listening. When listening is their goal, they make it *the* priority. They do not let *anything* distract.

Protégés feel the relationship is safe when mentors demonstrate receptivity and validation of their feelings. The goal is empathetic identification. The "I am the same as you" gesture promotes kinship and closeness vital to trust. Strength comes through the "I have been there as well" identification.

Reflective responses can be as simple as a short personal story that lets your protégé know you appreciate his or her feelings. Mildly self-deprecating anecdotes can be particularly solid boons to acceptance. Above all, acceptance is best served by humility and sensitivity. If you feel awkward, say you do. If you feel excited, say so. The sooner you verbalize your feelings, the faster the protégé will demonstrate matching vulnerability.

Mentors do not just listen, they listen dramatically. They demonstrate through their words and actions that the words of their protégés are valued and important. When people feel heard, they feel valued. Feeling valued, they are more likely to take risks and experiment. Only through trying new steps do they grow and learn. The bottom line is this: If your goal is to be a great mentor, start by using your noise-management skills to help you fully use your talents as a great listener.

Stage 3: Giving learning gifts of advice and feedback. Leveling the learning field and fostering acceptance and safety are the stages that lay the groundwork for the main event: giving learning gifts. Great mentors give many gifts—support, focus, courage, affirmation. But two crucial learning gifts are advice and feedback. Let's look briefly at each, starting with advice.

• *Advice.* Someone once asked famed, retired Notre Dame head football coach Lou Holtz what he considered to be the toughest part of his job. With his typical "aw shucks" charm, he finessed the question, but ultimately communicated that *one* of the hardest parts was "teaching lessons that stay taught." Mentors have a similar challenge. Protégé resistance and resentment to the mentor's advice and feedback creates the challenge in "teaching lessons that stay taught." As one frustrated supervisor commented, "I tell them what they ought to do, but it seems to go in one ear and out the other!"

Begin your advice giving by letting the protégé know the focus or intent of your mentoring. It sounds like this: "George, I wanted to talk with you about the fact that your last quarter call rate was up, but your sales were down 20 percent." For your advice to be received an applied, you need to be very specific and clear in your statement. Ambiguity clouds the conversation and risks leaving the protégé more confused than assisted.

Make certain that the protégé is as eager to improve or learn as you are to see him or her improve or learn. What do you do if you determine something the protégé needs to learn and the protégé either disagrees that learning is needed or is unwilling to learn what you want to teach? Take a broader perspective. If performance is a factor, be sure to have objective information ready (as a tool, not as proof). It is helpful in collectively examining needs. If all else fails, delay the conversation to a time when the protégé demonstrates a greater readiness to learn.

Ask permission to give advice. This is the most important step. Your goal at this point is twofold: 1) to communicate advice without surfacing protégé resistance, and 2) to keep ownership of the challenge with the protégé. It sounds like this: "I have some ideas on how you might improve, if that would be helpful to you." Remember, the goal is to communicate in a way that minimizes making the protégé feel controlled. State your advice in first-person singular. Phrases like "you ought to" quickly raise listener resistance. By keeping your advice in first-person singular—"what I've found helpful" or "what worked for me" —helps eliminate the "should's" and "ought to's." The protégé will hear such advice without the internal noise of resistance.

• **Feedback.** As advice is about *adding information*, feedback is fundamentally about *filling a blind spot*. And the "blindness" factor makes protégé feedback a tricky gift. How does a mentor bestow a gift that by its basic nature reminds the protégé of his or her inability to see it? How do you fill a perceptual gap and have the recipient focus on the gift, not the gap—to focus on the filled side of a filled hole?

The mentor's goal is to enhance the protégé's receptivity for feedback by creating a climate of identification. Seek comments that have an "I'm like you, that is, not perfect or flawless" kind of message. This need not be a major production or overdone, just a sentence or two.

State the rationale for your feedback. This is not a plea for subtlety or diplomacy as much as a petition for creating a readiness for gap filling. Help the protégé gain a clear sense of why the feedback is being given. Assume that you want to give feedback, and never have the protégé wondering, "Why is he/she telling me this?" or "How in the world can I benefit from this feedback?"

Assume you are giving *you* the feedback. We know that we more accurately hear feedback delivered in a fashion that is sensitive and unambiguous. However, there is another key dimension to giving effective feedback. Your feedback should possess the utmost integrity. This means it is straight and honest. Frankness is not about cruelty; it is about ensuring that the receiver does not walk away wondering, "What did he or she not tell me, that I needed to hear?" Think of your goal this way: How would you deliver the feedback if you were giving yourself the feedback? Take your cue from your own preferences.

It is instructive that the word "feedback" starts with the word "feed." Truly, the best gap filling is that which happens in the spirit of feeding or nurturing.

It is also fitting to know that the word "advice" probably originated from the Latin word "concilium," meaning "to call together." Our words "counsel" and "consult" have the same origin. If we blend these archaic definitions of "feedback" and "advice," we get a perfect description of a learning partnership—"to feed together."

Stage 4: Bolstering self-direction and independence. "Where is the 'good' in goodbye?" ask about a dozen pop songs. The message reminds us of what William Shakespeare wrote so long ago: "parting is such sweet sorrow." All mentoring relationships must come to an end. How do we manage a "farewell" with a focus on "well?"

Effective mentoring relationships are rich, engaging, and intimate. As such, ending them is not without emotion. No matter how hard we may try, there is a bittersweet dimension. However, healthy mentoring relationships craft separation as a tool for growth. Effective adjournment of the present mentoring relationship paves the way for effective inauguration of the next mentoring relationship.

Celebrate the relationship with fanfare and stories. A celebration need not be a party with band and banner. Celebration can be as simple as a special meal together, a drink after work, or a peaceful walk in a nearby park. The point of celebration is that it be clearly an event associated with the closure of the mentoring relationship. The rite of passage is a powerful symbol in gaining closure and moving on to the next learning plateau.

Celebration should include compliments and stories. Weave the celebration with laughter and joy. Your protégé now needs your blessing far more than your brilliance, and your well wishing more than your warnings. Avoid the temptation to lay out one last caution. Your kindest contribution will be a solid send off rendered with confidence, compassion, and consideration. Lace your final meeting or two with opportunities to remember, reflect, and refocus. Let your recall questions bridge the discussion toward the future.

Let some time pass before following up. The quickest route to delivering a message of dependence is to follow up with a protégé too soon after departure. Let at least a week pass before calling or visiting, maybe longer. Setting your relationship free requires a space of time. Should you follow up at all? Absolutely! Partners follow up on partners. The key is, not too quickly. Allow weaning time.

Letting go is rarely comfortable, but a thoughtful adjournment is always necessary to enable the protégé to flourish and continue to grow out of the shadow of a mentor—to become a self-directed learner. In the final analysis, the product of growing is "grown," which implies closure and culmination. Mark the moment by managing the adjournment of your relationship as a visible expression of achievement and happiness.

There is an expression in golf of "playing over your head." It means that a golfer is playing at an unexplained level of excellence in which serendipity and the extraordinary seem the momentary norm. Effective mentoring is a relationship of a mentor and protégé who seek to honor their alliance by "learning over their heads." Such an occurrence is practiced at its most harmonious level when the two "sing" as a partnership.

19

THE LOVE LEADER AS PASSION BEARER

L arry Smith lost it. And of all places, he lost it in the big-deal, quarterly executive meeting.

He absolutely went over the edge in his impassioned plea for some issue about a customer. No, he didn't cry, although he did wipe his eyes before his cheeks got streaked. No, he didn't pound the table, although he did demonstrate a few gestures that would be the envy of any aspiring thespian. But what Larry did do in his "out of control" passion clearly crossed all normal bounds of rationality and routine boardroom decorum. And yet, he engaged the hearts, and commitment, of every person in the meeting. People were truly moved. And it *did* make a difference. Stuff happened.

The "Larry loses his cool" incident led me to reflect on the true meaning of contemporary leadership, especially in a customer-love culture. I thought about how much "in charge"-land contained artifacts of control, rationality, and "keeping your cool." None of these relics seemed to go with the "L" word. I thought about how little these artifacts had anything to do with spirit and passion in *any* other context of life, except corporate life.

People do not brag about their rational marriage, their reasonable hobby, or their sensible vacation. There is rarely "in control" behavior when your daughter scores a goal or your son hits a home run. Exhortations of ecstasy are never restrained on the fishing bank when the cork suddenly disappears, and with surprising force. But somehow, all that spirit is an unwelcomed distraction at work. And the closer one gets to mahogany row, the less tolerance there seems to be for the "sounds of the heart."

I thought about how freeing it was for everyone in the room when "Larry lost his cool." Were we uncomfortable? Yes. Did we wonder, "Where the heck is this going?" Yes. But we all felt momentarily in kinship with *real* life. At the risk of sounding morbid, it was like the famous moth-and-flame poem. That's the one where the poet describes the predictable dance of moth and flame and ends by commenting about "that moth feeling more alive in that final moment than I have ever felt in my life." Julia Roberts echoed the same theme in *Steel Magnolias* when, as a courageous and passionate, diabetic expectant mother, facing the life-threatening potential of giving birth, she said, "I had rather have 30 minutes of "wonderful" than a lifetime of "nothing special."

Leaders are not rational beings; they are flame seekers. They passionately "give birth" in the face of threatening circumstance. The biography of almost every great leader who ever faced the potential of bodily harm accompanying his or her cause communicates a consistent theme: "*Why* we were there played so loud in my ear that I never really heard *what* might happen because we were there." Passion played, and leaders put issues like "in control" on some emotional back burner. We know Larry. And Larry is *not* an irrational, illogical person. Yet, somehow we trusted his passion more than his reason.

PASSION IS HONEST

I know I'm going to step into a philosophical room full of naysayerswith this comment. Here it is: Passion is more honest than reason. There it is. Out in the open. To be sure, logic is more elegant, more sensible, and surely more prudent. And one feels far more secure and calm with the rational. Predictability never makes the heart race. Passion leaves a person feeling fearful of the on-the-edge, unanticipated outcome. It also makes us feel free, alive, and somehow "a real, whole person." And when leaders surface that feeling in us, we are somehow more energized, like a knight ready for battle.

When I was an infantry unit leader in Vietnam, young men were observed going into battle with no knowledge of the complex socio-political ramifications of the Vietnam war. Yet, these men were ready to die. For what? For "duty, honor, and country." How illogical and amorphous can you get? What is the sensibility of courageously charging into a well-entrenched sniper, with an almost certain potential you will be among his body count, for duty? Where is the sensibility of bleeding on a rice paddy far from Cincinnati or Charlotte, for honor? What made GIs from McRae, Georgia, or Sterling, Illinois, get silver medals and distinguished whatevers? It was passion, not reason. Action was enticed by the spirit of the day, not the sanity of the moment. What would you die for at work? Is not business welfare as important to our global survival as national pride?

"Whoa!" you say. We can't have the chaos of unbridled emotion and the confusion of out-of-control desire. What would the stockholders say? After all, is it not the role of a leader to elicit a sense of "grace under pressure," or "order when all around you are loosing their heads"? Should leaders not strive to be more anchor than sail, more rudder than oar?

No! And again, no!

We have missed the boat on what it means to be a leader. The world, the organization, and the situation offer far more "predictable" than is predictably required. The truth is that rationality oozes from the seams of every business encounter. Leaders do not have to bring order, sanity, rationality, or logic. Every dimension of business life reeks with those qualities. Sane leaders foster insane passion. Memorable leaders call up in each of us a visit with the raggedy edge of brilliance and the out-of-the-way corner of genius. When we feel inspired, incensed, or ennobled, we have visited the magical realm of passion. And we typically return from that realm renewed, revitalized, and slightly revolted. The bittersweet taste of unexplored talent is the byproduct of a passion projection into that world. And when a leader has a hand in that flight, there is at once a sense of security wedded to an otherwise solitary search.

PASSION IS INVITATIONAL

Passionate connections provoke passionate responses. When leaders "pass-I-on" to another, it triggers a "pass-me-back" response. And leadership is fundamentally about influencing. Ask 20 people to name the greatest leaders of all times. Sure, you might get a military general or two. But the list will likely be made up of leaders who stirred their followers with fire more than leaders who lectured their followers with reasoning. Kennedy, Churchill, King, Teresa, Schweitzer, and Gandhi were not famous for their rationalism, nor is Southwest Airlines CEO Herb Kelleher, Bruce Nordstrom, the late Sam Walton, or the late J. Willard Marriott, Sr. Leaders' invitations to action are embossed on their own yearnings to express their "cause" to others in ways that encourage others to join.

PASSION IS MAGICAL

Passion takes the plain vanilla out of encounters. It is a leap into relationships. And it is magical. The poet Goethe called it "boldness." He said, "Whatever you can do, or dream you can, begin in boldness. Boldness has genius, power, and magic in it. Until one is committed, there is hesitancy, the chance to draw back, always ineffectiveness. The moment one definitely commits oneself, then Providence moves, too. All sorts of things occur to help one that would never otherwise have occurred."

Philosopher Hegel wrote, "Nothing great in the world has been accomplished without passion."

Followers need passionate connections. Leaders who come soaring from the heart awaken boldness in others. It builds a relationship platform that raises everyone to a higher level. Southern Civil War General Thomas J. Jackson was never again called "Tom" after someone spotted him on the battlefield and remarked, "There stands General Jackson, like a stone wall." His troops developed the reputation of demonstrating the same spirited, "never say die" passion in combat. And who can forget the same phenomenon among leaders named Martin, Mahatma, and Susan B.? Again, people may be instructed by reason, but they are inspired by passion.

Why are you here, in this role, at this time? What difference will your being here make? What legacy will you leave behind? Will you be forgotten for what you maintained, or remembered for what you added? Imposing mountains are climbed, culture-changing movements are started, and breakthrough miracles are sparked by leaders who take off the restraints of rationalism and prudence, letting their spirit ascend from within.

20

THE LOVE LEADER AS CHANGE AGENT

Do some people in your organization resist change? Who are you going to call? Bring in the resistance busters to exterminate those resistance pests!

Making change happen in organizations would be a lot easier if there weren't those pesky resisters. There are the openly angry types, filled with long memories of pain and loud messages of blame. There are the pessimistic, "it'll never fly" types who would throw a wet blanket on the most carefully planned party. Finally, there are the silent grumps who never actually say anything; they just roll their eyes skyward, cross their arms defiantly, and slowly shake their heads from side to side.

People don't resist change. People resist what they believe will result in pain, over which they have no control. Rather than eliminating pests, wise organizations manage change so that the pests never show up.

The idea that "People resist what they believe" implies that resistance begins with a vision or picture. When people sense change in the wind, they assess its potential impact based on what they know, what they've heard, and what they've experienced. Without any information, some simply react to the fear of the unknown. As one person sees the unknown as an adversary, another sees it as an adventure. Again, what they have experienced tells them whether to be cautious of the unknown, or whether to courageously embrace the unknown.

"This will result in pain" suggests a person's belief is that the change will be associated with something painful. "Pain" may be loss of job, loss of status, or loss of influence. It can also mean the pain of rejection, looking stupid, or losing contact with important relationships. Part of effective change management includes getting a clear sense of what "pain" represents to the people impacted by the change.

Often it is not *pain* we resist, but rather pain over which we have no control or influence. That annual, New Year's "get in shape" resolution always carries some pain. We know it; we expect it; and we have control of the resolution. Control implies a belief that we will not be a victim of the change, that we will shape the change, or at least shape how we are impacted by the change.

FIVE KEYS OF CHANGE MANAGEMENT

Every part of the definition of resistance to change represents one important factor of change management. If "perception" is a key factor in resistance, for instance, then extraordinary communication becomes a key strategy for overcoming resistance. If "control" is a key factor of resistance, then inclusion becomes a vital strategy of change management. Likewise, if "pain" is part of keeping people on the sidelines, then compassionate role models are the tools for getting resisters in the game.

The architecture of change management involves five keys, which are reflected in the model below.

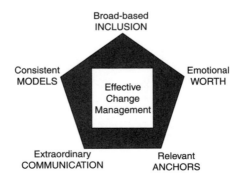

Each of these elements answers a key concern expressed by people resisting change.

1. Broad-based inclusion: "They Don't Care What We Think." This expression of resistance generally contains an element of truth. Most organizations have historically been long on pronouncement and short on participation. And the more top-down, "now hear this" decisions are made, the more the we-they schism is fueled. Inclusion works magic on all relationships—especially when change is needed. Employees reward with their commitment those organizations that treat them like partners.

Effective change management requires broad-based inclusion or participation. The ancient adage "people will care if they share" has great truth. While few employees expect any organization to "let us run the place," they do expect to be trusted enough to be asked for their input in those areas that matter to them and where their input has value. With participation comes creativity and commitment. Sustainable change will only occur if it has a widespread "we" approach. It is difficult to feel "victim" when one has a hand in crafting the outcome. Through inclusion, they share control.

2. Emotional worth: "What's in it for me." People are not inherently selfish when they ask, "What's in it for me?" However, they clearly choose where to put their efforts based on what they perceive as worthy of those efforts. Effective change management requires ensuring that there is a clearly perceived link between their effort and some outcome people believe has emotional worth.

Worth comes in many forms—economic, affirmation, growth, status, power. However, the root of worth lies in the degree to which it has emotional grounding (or it matters deeply to the person). Smart organizations help employees see the direct link between required change and competitive survival. They help employees understand that a winning organization is one that is adaptive, responsive, and perpetually in sync with the needs of its marketplace. This requires associates who are anxious to grow, hungry to improve, and enthusiastic about retaining an edge of excellence. It helps people see the "what's in it for me" side of the change.

3. Relevant anchors. "This too will pass." Organizations have been weathering monumental change for a long time. And given the short-term attention span of most organizations, employees have typically seen many change efforts come and go. The byproduct is twofold. First, employees who are experienced with what Ron Zemke calls the "BOHICA" syndrome ("bend over, here it comes again") have developed great facility at stoically resisting until it all blows over. "Just wait," they tell newer, more naive employees. "The shine will wear off on this 'management by bestseller' effort. Before long, there will be another banner and another battle cry trumpeting the newest quick fix." Second, as employees' cynicism gets more embedded, their attitudes grow more calloused. The more energy an organization devotes to convincing, the more energy they devote to contesting.

The effective change management antidote to the "BOHICA" syndrome is to take actions that in time convince even the most ardent cynic that the change effort is not going away. This means the change must have relevant anchors. It means the change must not be perceived as an add-on effort. *Effective change management* means that the change is deliberately hard-wired into the norms, values, mores, and symbols of the organization. *Relevant* means the anchors are those that capture the attention of employees and are deemed important. When the incentive system is altered to reflect the change effort, when the champions of change are the people getting the best assignments or promotions, or when executive leaders frequently ask for status reports on the change efforts, relevance is being communicated.

Often, change fails to be sustained because it is seen as a project or program—something outside of or separate from the normal flow of work. Therefore, sustainable change must be embedded in the folklore, language, and rituals of the organization. For example, if change is needed, but not anchored in the organization's rewards system, it will likely not last. If change is needed, but it is not an integral part of the person's daily work patterns (like a topic on the agenda of most every meeting, or wired into the standards of the organization), it will not be sustained.

4. Extraordinary communication. "Psst...Have You Heard That?" There is an old *Peanuts* strip in which the teacher asks Lucy, "What is 3 + 4?" Lucy does not know the answer. The teacher tests Lucy again: "What is 4 + 8?" Again, Lucy comes up blank. A third time the teacher asks, "What is 5 + 2?" In desperation to save face in front of her peers, Lucy answers, "I don't know. But I can spell 'Mississippi!'"

Rumors and myths get started that way. Rarely are rumors sparked by malicious intent. Most often, they begin with the kind of pressure Lucy felt. When people are expected to know and do not know, they often save face by concocting what they believe the truth to be. And few things derail worthy change like a falsehood fervently believed. As the anxiety of change increases, people will "spell Mississippi" when they can't do the math.

Effective change management requires extraordinary communication. Any change effort fuels rumors and myths. The best remedy for erroneous information is communication—both in terms of the information disseminated and the feedback sought and given. As people get the information they need, their resistance is quelled as they develop perceptions of the future that are less painful than they imagined. Communication must take many forms, must be constant, and above all, must be candid and frank.

5. Consistent models: "They don't walk the talk." Effective change management requires consistent models—actions by people seen by employees as holding the greatest influence. In most organizations, the influencers are the leaders, particularly at the top. People take their cue about a change effort's importance from witnessing leaders who are behaving consistently with the needed change. People are leader watchers. This means all the actions, behaviors, and priorities of leaders must be consistent (over time) and congruent with the change effort.

There will always be resistance around any important change efforts. It is important to remember what Price Pritchett and Ron Pound call the *20-50-30 Rule*: 20 percent of any population are early endorses of change, anxious to embrace progress; 30 percent will be anti-change and are likely to resist no matter what actions are taken. The leadership focus should be on the 50 percent "fence sitters"—those early resisters who, with effective change management, could join the endorsers.

21

REINVENTING SERVICE WITH LOVE IN MIND

What do Bill Marriott, Fred Smith, Debbi Fields, and Al Hopkins have in common? No, they're not all rich and famous! In fact, Al is a small town-preacher in South Georgia. They all are (or were) innovators in ways to better service customers.

J. Willard (Bill, Sr.) Marriott in 1927 noticed that people at Hoover Airport (now Ronald Reagan National) were going past his small Hot Shoppe restaurant near the airport and buying take-out food before boarding an Eastern Airlines flight. Bill started the first food catering service to airlines for meals on board.

Fred Smith was the founder of Federal Express. On his Yale College research paper on how to create an overnight air freight business, he received a grade of "C", along with a note from the professor that explained the low grade: Fred's concept was "clever, but an impractical concept." We know the rest of the story.

Debbi Fields saw the growing popularity of shopping malls. She created a computer hookup with each mall-based cookie stand that enabled the operator to make smart decisions by the hour on what cookies to offer and which to discount.

And Al Hopkins? He watched the other 10-year-olds in his neighborhood wait for customers to stop by their sidewalk lemonade stand. Al abandoned the "stand" concept and took his small lemonade business door-to-door. He made enough money in one summer to buy a new Schwinn Flyer.

Innovative customer service is all about seeing what other people see, but thinking about new applications. The losers are those who stick with "our way." For instance, television was not started by the big movie studios, trucking was not started by the firmly planted railroad industry, and the first motels came from upstarts like Holiday Inn, not grand hotel giants like Hilton. Innovation starts with challenging assumptions about every aspect of the service experience.

But it also includes staying clear on what customers like and need. FedEx spent a ton of money with "zap-mail." It was to work like this: A courier would pick up your correspondence, take it to a FedEx office, and fax it to the destination city, where a courier on the other end would deliver faxed copy minutes later to the intended receiver. FedEx missed the mark because it never realized that fax machines would become so inexpensive that customers would buy their own.

Some people are naturally creative; most of us are not. And our brains don't help us, given the way they work. Brains are basically information organizers. Since far more data comes into our brains than we can handle, brains look for patterns to accept, sort, and save information. The good news is that brain patterns save us tons of time. You have a whole pattern in your brain called "Watergate" or "Overhaul" or "World Series." You don't have to hear each part of the pattern each time. "Bridge out" causes us to stop without running off the edge—we complete the pattern in our brain and apply the brake.

However, patterns have their liability, especially when it comes to creativity. Ideas that seem like a part of an old pattern get prematurely shelved to that pattern in our brains. Patterns can make us rigid and self-righteous. Patterns can make us arrogant and closed. "We've always done it that way" or "That's just the way it's done" are clues of a pattern that has become an idea-stopper.

THREE PATTERN BUSTERS

The creativity techniques that follow are aimed at essentially tricking the brain by breaking the pattern. What can result are innovative applications of how to more effectively serve customers.

1. Why, Why, Why, What if . . . The childhood game of repeatedly asking "Why?" is an excellent way to start. Begin with some aspect of your organization, such as the customer's initial contact with the service department. Describe "what happens now," followed by the first "why," the answer, a second "why," the answer, and a third "why" and the answer. Then, consider a new application of the third answer—a "what if." To illustrate, let's try an example.

What happens now (with the customer's initial contact with the service department)? Answer: The customer walks in to the service department and up to a large counter for service check-in. *Why?* Answer: Because it keeps them out of the service-bay area. *Why?* Answer: So the service writer can be close to the computer for record keeping and invoicing. *Why?* Answer: Because it puts the customer in the waiting area so we can find them when their service work is completed.

What if . . . we gave service customers a smart card with all the information about their car's service record on it and allowed a greeter to meet them in their car. The greeter could take the smart card as customers describe their need or problem and could then give customers a small beeper to signal them when their car was ready. We could escort customers to our special entertainment and business center near the new car showroom. When customers are signaled that their car is ready for pick-up, we could make sure their smart card is updated and returned as they leave in their newly washed car.

2. Feelings benchmarking. A popular technique used by many organizations is benchmarking. It involves selecting some aspect of your business that you seek to improve, identifying the organizations that perform that aspect the best, and then arranging

153

to visit the "best of the best" to learn how they do what they do. If your organization was looking at starting a telemarketing call center, you might visit L.L. Bean or Land's End. If you were thinking of putting in a customer-record system, you might look at USAA insurance or Ritz Carlton Hotels.

There is another approach to benchmarking called "feelings benchmarking." Instead of benchmarking best practices, it involves looking at your service through the "eyes" of a service provider who is famous for making customers feel the way you want your customers to feel.

First, identify a part of your customer's service experience that might benefit from a new approach. For example, you might chose the wait customers experience during a minor repair or maintenance.

Second, decide what you want your customer to feel at the end of that wait. Feelings or emotions are different from evaluations. FedEx, for example, works to make customers feel confident; Mary Kay Cosmetics works to make customers feel pampered; Ritz Carlton and Four Seasons Hotels works to make their guests feel "elite or rich." USAA insurance works to make customers feel "like family." Let's assume you decided you wanted your customers to feel "happy as a kid."

Third, select some service provider you know is superb at making their customers feel like you want your customers to feel. For example, If you want your customers to feel "happy as a kid," you might choose Disney, Chucky Cheese, or Stew Leonard's Dairy Store. Let's pretend you choose Disney.

Fourth, ask how the service hero you selected would reinvent the service challenge you picked to make customers feel the particular emotion you chose. In our example, this would mean asking, "How would Disney improve 'customer wait' to help customers feel 'happy as a kid.'" Obviously, we don't know what Disney would do, but we can probably guess. They might have special entertainment, video games, race car drivers come by and sign autographs, cartoon videos on car maintenance, magazines customers *say* they want, some way to let you keep track of how long you still have to wait, etc. The goal of this technique is to use "new eyes" to review your service delivery.

3. Attribute triggers. Many great service breakthroughs are born of innovator thinking, "What if we made it faster, cheaper, lighter, automated, etc.?" The goal is to identify some quality or attribute and apply it to some practice or application. Domino's was by no means the first pizza parlor that delivered pizza. But they perfected the thought about making it faster, and guaranteed it. Southwest Airlines was the first to perfect "Let's make it on time, every time, and cheaper." Kinko's was the first to perfect "around the clock" (and they've added "free pick-up and delivery").

Below is a list of attributes to be used as triggers for innovative service ideas. Even if your first thought is, "Naw, that's not relevant to us," try to think about what service would be like if you "forced" it to fit. You may be surprised at what you discover.

What if we designed how we give great service so that it was...

• Faster	• More fun	• Divided into parts
• Slower	• More inspirational	• Done with a guide
• Quicker	• More instructional	• Done with a manual
• Longer	• More inclusive	• Done anywhere/remotely
• Smaller	• More invisible	• Done with something else
• Larger	• More elegant/Classy	• Done automatically
• Cheaper	• More responsive	• Completely tailored
• Bolder	• More attractive	• Done backward
• Funnier	• More efficient	• Done while you wait

Customers are attracted—and remain loyal—to organizations with a bent for innovation. While they want the core values and substantive service offering to remain constant, they enjoy being positively surprised by novel enhancements and refreshing improvements. As customers, we are bored easily. And the antidote to boredom is a climate teeming with excitement that is propagated by service providers anxious to experiment.

CUSTOMER LOVE

22

HOMESTYLE CUSTOMER LOVE

The torrential rain kept me from jogging the city streets during the early morning hours as I had planned. And the health club of the St. Louis Pavilion Marriott where I was staying was very crowded. I elected to scrap my run and speed-walk the hallways of the 14th floor, on which my hotel room was located. The 30-minute walk up and down the same long, carpeted halls gave me as much education as it did exercise.

The St. Louis Pavilion Marriott is an old, but elegant hotel situated close beside Busch Stadium—so close that I had watched the last three innings of the St. Louis Cardinals-Houston game from my room on the evening I arrived. But it is more than baseball, beer, and a view of the Mississippi that brings patrons back time and again to this hotel. It is world-class service that begins in the early morning hours in quiet corners and back-of-the-house crannies.

"I'll help you with that," I heard one housekeeper call to another as I rounded the corner on my hallway speed walk. "Good morning, I'm so glad to see you," I heard a room service attendant say to a hotel security person as they met near the elevator. "Just leave it in my area, and I'll be delighted to repair it for you," said a hotel engineer to a housekeeper who was holding a broken iron. The tone of each of them was warm, enthusiastic, and grateful for the opportunity to serve. It reminded me of a homestyle meal—folksy, generous, and inclusive.

Customer love begins and ends with the front-line experience. Customers return with their friends and their funds if they get customer service that is responsive, reliable, resourceful, and personal. And most customers believe that the experience at the front line is a peep hole into the entire organization. The source of external customer loyalty is internal customer loyalty. A surly front-line person can mean to the customer that the organization is not a very nice place to work. An incompetent service person says the organization doesn't care enough to provide adequate employee training. Marriott Hotels found that a 5 percent reduction in turnover increased guest repeats by 10 percent and profits by more than $150 million. Great service providers have found that the number one impact on customer relations is employee relations.

Creating a customer devotion culture is clearly the responsibility of the manager, supervisor, or owner. However, it is also the responsibility of the front-line service person. Everyone likes to cop out with, "This place would be better if top management would . . . " And as true as the statement may be, it is far from complete. Culture building takes everyone, not just those in the front office. A customer-love culture requires the collective efforts of every professional in the organization. And it is particularly dependent on the front-line person.

The service person should be a role model of great service to other employees. To repeat Will Rogers' famous saying, "People learn from observation, not conversation." While Will was referring to politicians, the message is just as clear for service people. Associates do not watch your mouth; they watch your moves—the actions you take with customers and the actions you take with other associates. Few practices create a customer-love culture more than walking the talk.

THE RECIPE FOR HOMESTYLE

How does a front-line service person nurture and support a customer-love culture? How do we create that homestyle service that causes customers to feel attracted to the organization? What are the ways we keep our organization focused on customer devotion?

When I was growing up, my grandmother had an old recipe for rabbit stew—a delicacy she served only on special occasions. Written in longhand and passed down from her ancestry, the recipe started with a provocative, but practical beginning step: "First, get a rabbit!" Just like making rabbit stew, homestyle service begins with the most basic ingredient—the organization. Homestyle starts at home, the source of customer devotion.

1. Customer service begins at "home." Customers will feel like love only to the degree they experience love happening within the organization. Jan Carlzon, former CEO of Scandinavian Airlines, was fond of saying, "If you aren't serving your customer, your job is to be serving someone who is." This means striving to give your colleagues the same level of service you endeavor to give customers. It means being patient, tolerant, and forgiving of associates, just like we are (or should be) with customers of the organization.

Members of a healthy, fully functioning family feel jointly responsible to each other, know how to trade on each others' strengths, and are committed to collective success. Just as in a healthy family, interdependent actions among employees give customers a sense of confidence; mutual commitments to each other show customers a sense of joy. Great teamwork not only means the "right hand knows what the left hand is doing" but it also means "the right hand *cares* about what the left hand is doing."

Look for ways to lend a helping hand. Let go of the "tit for tat" ("you scratch my back and I'll scratch yours") kind of attitude. Support your associates because they are your partners, not to get anything back. Never "go the extra mile" as a form of bribery—"I have given you something special, now I expect you to respond with your allegiance." This can cause your associates to feel the tug of guilt akin to the one we sometimes feel if we get a wedding or graduation invitation from someone we barely know and elect not to send a present. Guilt-based relationships are *not* healthy relationships.

Think about it. What happens in other relationships when you give with an "other" (rather than self) focus? How are other relationships in your life altered by beneficial gestures free of any "what's in it for me"?

Try something. Starting today, select an associate you enjoy and feel proud to have as an associate in your organization. Think about a gift you might give. Think of personal favors before you consider tangible objects. Now, when you've finished planning for a favorite associate, select an associate you do not particularly enjoy and almost wish you didn't have as an associate. Take the exact same approach as you did with the one you like. The specific gifts may be different, but the approach should be the same. After one month, examine how the relationship has changed. Then, decide if the "giver" orientation is more powerful than the "give to get" orientation to service. That's homestyle customer service in its purest form.

2. *Homestyle service is fueled by a smile.* The ingredient every homestyle recipe contains is fun. Homestyle cooked meals are generally joyfully prepared meals. Restaurants put the phrase "homestyle" in front of fun foods, like barbecue, chili, and fried chicken. Homestyle wine or beer usually carries bragging rights at the first uncorking with friends and family. Somewhere woven into the concept of *homestyle* is the element of festivity and delight. The organization should be no different.

"What do you like most about working here?" I asked employees at the St. Louis Pavilion Marriott. "We have fun!" was the most frequent answer I received. Research continually shows that organizations that promote fun have higher productivity, morale, and customer satisfaction. Ever see an unhappy employee at Disney, Southwest Airlines, Home Depot? And check out their bottom line! Happy company turnover and absenteeism are considerably lower. Did you know that a hearty belly laugh can actually make you immune to most diseases for almost an hour? That means that if you laughed every hour, you'd probably never get sick!

Look for events to celebrate. Find actions that make you happy and that make your work environment cheerful. I have a friend who wears a Superman t-shirt under his three-piece business suit when he knows he's facing a tough day at the office. Wire flowers to yourself. Find a favorite cartoon and put it near your work area. Do one mischievous, playful activity a week designed to lighten up your associates. Treat an associate to lunch and agree *not* to talk about work. Send a thank-you note to an associate who least expects it. And if you really want to have some fun, next time you are in a toll lane, pay the toll for the car behind you and then don't let them catch up to see who you are.

Remember to give your associates lots of sincere compliments and affirmations. Think of genuine affirmation as giving people a kind of emotional bullet-proof vest. When front-line employees encounter the occasional difficult and irate customers, "bullet-proof vests" enable them to survive the situation without their spirits sagging. Sherry McCool, general manager of the St. Louis Pavilion Marriott, says, "One of our key values is to 'celebrate our excellent efforts (even if they didn't all work out) as well as our successes.' We started celebrating a lot more when we saw the power that having fun had on our resilience to provide high-quality service consistently to our guests and associates."

3. Homestyle service is sustained by passion. There are many things about a customer encounter over which service advisers have no control. However, the one thing they *do* control is how they elect to react. And front-line people who pursue customer love are not afraid to show their passion for customers and the honor of getting to build long-term customer loyalty. Homestyle *anything* is concocted with far more heart (passion) than head (logic).

Customers enjoy dealing with people who show an unbridled passion about their associates and their customers. Watch Herb Kelleher, CEO of Southwest Airlines, working side by side with associates on the tarmac, loading luggage on a busy holiday. See Cindy Fields, CEO of Victoria's Secret Catalog, sitting beside a front-line fashion consultant, helping a call-in customer select lingerie. Ride with Rich Teerlink, CEO of Harley-Davidson, as he visits dealers in an effort to learn their needs and expectations of corporate headquarters in Milwaukee. Follow Sherry McCool around at the St. Louis Pavilion Marriott, and notice the impact of her infectious smile. All four of these people share one thing in common (which they loudly demonstrate)—an almost embarrassing level of passion and devotion to customers.

When was the last time your associates saw you giggle over some incident, show humility over an error, or get misty-eyed over a heart-tugging action? "One person with passion," wrote E. B. Forster, "is better than 40 people merely interested." And to repeat, Hegel wrote, "Nothing great in the world has been accomplished without passion." Herb, Cindy, Rich, and Sherry would agree.

4. Homestyle Service Ends with "Thanks." Thanking the customer is important; thanking our associates is even more important. One thing I noticed that happened frequently at the St. Louis Pavilion Marriott was the sincere and assertive manner the associates used to thank each other. When customers are in an environment of gratitude, they feel valued.

Saying "thanks" is a great start. But take one more step. Let the person you are thanking know exactly what he or she did to warrant your gratitude. The story behind the credit is important. For example, when my wife and I were eating at a local restaurant, our waiter had a name tag plus an additional tag proclaiming him as the "employee of the month." "Congratulations, I see you are the 'employee of the month," my wife said to him. "What did you do to warrant such an honor?" The waiter stood quietly for a moment and then said flatly, "I guess it was my turn." He had no idea what he had done to be recognized, so he knew of no special action he was being encouraged to repeat.

The success of a customer-love strategy depends on the commitment of the front-line person who goes the extra mile in nurturing customer loyalty. It happens when service people demonstrate the same service-oriented attitude toward colleagues thatthey do toward customers. It happens when service people say (and live): "If it is to be, it must begin with me."

23

How the Customer Gets Love

By reading this book, you are—I hope—gaining helpful insights and useful tools for creating and sustaining customer devotion. However, you are also a customer. How do you get service providers to treat you as if they care about your loyalty? That important question reminds me of Jimmie Steele.

Jimmie Steele is a world-class real estate agent in Mint Hill, North Carolina. He also is a world-class customer who gets terrific service wherever he goes. He has a knack for getting the best table, best hotel room, upgraded airline seats, and complimentary everything. I even witnessed a local hardware dealer give Jimmie his coat when he overheard Jimmie's wife, Karen, comment that she was a little cold. Not a loan, mind you. A gift!

Six Secrets to Receiving Customer Love

Here are six of the Steele secrets.

1. Check your attitude before the door. Jimmie believes he deserves great service, and he acts that way. This does not mean he goes in throwing his weight around and making demands. It means he enters the scene with an expectation that greatness is about to happen, that it is about to happen to him, and that it *should* happen to him. He actually visualizes being served well. His mental picture, confident expectation, and enthusiastic anticipation create a self-fulfilling prophecy that almost never fails to materialize.

165

2. *Carefully manage the first 10 seconds.* Jimmie is by nature a happy, optimistic guy. And when he enters an opportunity for service, he turns his infectious warmth up about 10 degrees. He knows that the first 10 seconds of any encounter are key to shaping the reception he is likely to get. He aims his Rolls Royce smile at the service provider and creates a greeting that loudly says, "We are about to have some unbelievable fun here. And you are invited!" Jimmie is a living example of "Give the world the best you have, and the best will come back to you."

3. *Help the Service Provider Give You Greatness.* Jimmie believes 99.9 percent of the people in service roles are eager to give great service. But sometimes there are barriers that make giving greatness difficult. Jimmie is always a willing helper in clearing them away. If the barrier happens to be a foul mood, Jimmie is there with a quick tease, a sincere compliment, or a thoughtful condolence to transform sour face into sunny. If the barrier is a silly policy, Jimmie has a creative suggestion that helps him meet his need without putting the service provider at risk. Jimmie is always willing to invest added time at the beginning of the transaction for a rich return in the end.

4. *Always lace your encounters with respect.* No matter how sullen the service provider or how determined the provider to provide the bare minimum, Jimmie treats every service provider with respect. He is wise enough to know that sometimes a "no" is an unshakable "no." He is always assertive, but never aggressive, pushy, or demanding. He just brings out his best Sunday manners, loaded with the words "please," "sir," and "thank you." I have never seen this fail him. "Sometimes people really want to be angry, and they resent someone trying to force them to give it up," he told me one day. "I found that if you treat them with obvious respect, even if they are cantankerous, they don't see you as coercing them into giving up their attitude. Then, that's what they end up doing. They give up trying to be grumpy."

5. Invite the service provider to join in your adventure.
With Jimmie, life always seems like the festivities are about to start. He has an impish style that lets service providers let themselves be a little mischievous. He is crystal clear to them regarding his goal; he is obvious about his intent and enthusiastic about the possibilities. A typical person might simply announce, "I'd like a non-smoking table with a view, please." Not Jimmie! He starts off with, "Boy, this is gonna be one special night. And we are so lucky to be here!" Then, he outlines his goal. "We'd love to get the table *you'd* want if this was your special night. We know you can get us the right spot." Then, he turns to his family or friends with a line like, "Hey, we might order champagne" or "I can taste that thick steak already," or simply "Isn't this exciting?" Instead of just reciting a dinner order, Jimmie sometimes describes the type of meal he'd like, asks the waiter to choose it, and closes with "and surprise me!" He not only gets great choices, but waiters go out of their way to ensure that their choice worked for him. And they always do.

6. Be generous and thoughtful. Jimmie never views a service encounter as a single transaction. It is always the start of an important relationship. Since he assumes he'll be back, he is generous in expressing his gratitude for great service. He is quick to recommend a good service provider to a colleague. He remembers great service providers who serve him well, sending them notes, articles, cards. He is ready to help them out when they are experiencing difficulties, like the time his laundry was going through a tough period after the owner died and his wife and son were struggling to keep the business going. Jimmie managed to work their story into his Sunday School report, and almost half of the congregation took their cleaning to that laundry the next week. The windfall business got the family through a tight financial spot, thanks to Jimmie's special philanthropy.

Customer love is a two-way street. While loyalty is typically initiated from the service provider to the customer, it can also work the other way. Sometimes it is the customer who takes charge of elevating the relationship from "pretty good" to "I wouldn't go anywhere else." Steele Realty is a model of great service because the founder crafted the mold by heart. Jimmie Steele serves from the heart, and not surprisingly, he is served in the same fashion.

24

AFFIRMING CUSTOMER LOVE

Tony Lay was a Romeo! When he and I were roommates in college, he pursued a serious romance with my sister. On one occasion when he "came a-courting," he brought her a large bouquet of flowers. He also brought our mother a single red rose for her favorite bud vase. Needless to say, Tony got the green light when he popped the "may-I-have-your-daughter's-hand" question. And, my sister got affirmation she was marrying a boy with good manners. After thirty plus years of marriage to my sister, Tony still remembers his mother-in-law in little special ways.

If loyalty is the primary consequence of customer love, affirmation is its context. Love by definition is the display of affection. We show our love and we know we are loved through the spirit of affirmation. It is an unabashed declaration of preference; the antithesis of indifference. Customer love is both gained and retained through positive pronouncements.

Affirming customer love is a two-sided affair. Associates who pursue conduct that produces customer love need to be affirmed; customers who answer with their allegiance also need to be affirmed.

Much has been written about rewarding great service. Successful reward and recognition programs typically center on identifying and publicizing those behaviors that organizations deem should be emulated by others. Stories are told;

illustrations are provided; and both individual and team actions are celebrated.

Much has also been written about rewarding customer loyalty. Successful customer affinity programs center on identifying customers who return, profiling their preferences for more tailored treatment, and then incenting their allegiance through special attention, valued privileges and favorable economics. For example:

American Airlines treats their executive platinum passengers with tender loving care. When passengers pass the 100,000 air miles a year threshold, they are provided a secret toll-free number to access the "executive desk." Highly trained professionals staff the desk around the clock to do all manner of travel challenge problem solving. Should executive platinum passengers arrive at an airport with an extra-long walk to their connecting flight, a chauffeured motorized cart is often standing by to whisk them to the distant gate. Expensive ice cream toppings mailed to their home, special luggage tags, and no blackout times on frequent flyer free tickets all let these customers know their loyalty is appreciated.

The Tony Lay approach to affirming love, however, goes to a deeper level. It entails affirmation in stereo! It requires affirming the target as well as that target's target. Tony was not trying to butter up our mother for his own advantage…my sister STILL had to be home by 11pm. He simply recognized that our mother was an important component of my sister's life and therefore needed to be encompassed in his expression of adoration. Besides, his affection for our mother was (and is) authentic.

Think about your associates' world. Whom do they value? Is there a way to affirm their great customer service by encircling their loved ones in that expression? While it is important that we respect associates' privacy, creative inclusion may give your reward and recognition effort greater depth. A personal handwritten note to the family of someone who gave extraordinary effort might be more powerful than the proverbial rubber chicken awards banquet. Sending an employee to a training session taught by his or her hero, inviting an employee's neighbors to the service awards ceremony, recognizing her or him in front of important work colleagues (like YOUR manager), can send a message with much sweeter sounds than traditional recognition efforts.

Customers also can benefit from stereophonic affirmation. Who are your customer's customers? Are there ways to affirm your customer through your customer's customer? An investment management company that caters to brokerage firms provided their best clients a two-day learning experience at a resort. The invited account execs got a special bonus—they were encouraged to bring THEIR best client to the experience. The brokerage firms got affirmation from both ends...from the investment management company AND from that firms' customers who now saw their brokerage firm in a more esteemed way.

The caution of privacy is again important. Some customers are protective of their customers. In this era of disintermediaries (like Dell Computer) who eliminate all parties between the original manufacturer and the customer, there is particularly heightened caution about what could be perceived as an end run to eliminate the middle. Additionally, customers often have their own affirmation efforts underway and can resent being preempted. Approach the target's target in the spirit of partnership. Be candid about your motives to your customer and keep them, not their customer, in the driver's seat.

When customer love goes unaffirmed it risks sending a message of indifference. While giving great service can be its own reward, the absence of rewards for extra effort communicates it has a low priority. In time, employees lose pride and customers lose interest. Ultimately, customers (and employees) who feel their loyalty is taken for granted take their devotion elsewhere.

CUSTOMER LOVE

25

TWENTY FIVE WAYS TO
SHOW YOUR LOVE

Most customer relationships don't end in conflict. Most are neglected to death. Neglect is more dangerous than strife; indifference is more costly than error. Great relationships are fueled by affirmation. Nurturing the bounty of customer loyalty requires more than proper cultivation and seeding. It must be fertilized with attention and care.

Courting the customer does not end with the sale or transaction. Superior service providers never take a valued relationship for granted and remain ever vigil for ways to celebrate the joy of the partnership and express gratitude for the return it provides.

Here are 25 ways to show customer love. Use this list to jump start your own list. Amplify the items to suit your situation and customers. Remember, what works for one customer may be a turn off for another. Recognition comes from the root word *cognoscere* meaning "to know." Tailor your affirmation.

- Invite a customer to an important staff meeting.
- Arrange for a special learning experience for customers.
- Hand-write a thank-you note to a key customer.
- Send customers greeting cards on all key holidays.
- Name a policy, building, or conference room for a key customer.
- Provide a special parking space for a key customer.
- Start a fund or scholarship in the name of a key customer.

- Provide a donation in the name of your customer to his or her favorite charity.
- Provide a special discount for loyal customers.
- Create a forum that allows for public recognition of customers.
- Remember a customer's birthday in a unique and personalized way.
- Send customers a subscription to a magazine they value.
- Buy helpful books for key customers.
- Invite customers to your home for a cookout.
- Provide tickets to an event valued by the customer.
- Nominate your customer for a special award.
- Find a way to compliment your customer to their customer.
- Put up pictures of your customer in the cafeteria.
- Invite customers to your facility to talk about their needs and goals to all employees.
- Feature key customers in your organization's newsletter.
- Give your customer a gift you won.
- Poll your customers for their input on important changes you plan to make.
- Ask your customers for advice on how to better run your organization.
- Purchase an ad in a key publication to thank your customers.
- Have an executive write a thank-you letter to a key customer.

What's your favorite way to show customer love? I'd like to hear from you. I plan to give away a free book every week for the next year to the best idea on how to show customer love. Send your ideas to:

Chip R. Bell
Performance Research Assoc., Inc.
25 Highland Park #100
Dallas, TX 75205-2785
Phone: 214-522-5777
Fax: 214-691-7691
email: chip@beepbeep.com

BIBLIOGRAPHY

Page

9   *Discovering the Soul of Service*, Leonard L. Berry (New York: The Free Press, 1999).

10 *Customers as Partners: Building Relationships that Last*, Chip R. Bell, (San Francisco: Berrett-Koehler Publishers, 1994).

11 *Sea of Cortez: A Leisurely Journal of Travel and Research*, John Steinbeck and Edward F. Ricketts (New York: Viking Press, 1941), p. 2.

21 *Customers for Life: How to Turn That One-time Buyer into a Lifetime Customer*, Carl Sewell and Paul B. Brown, (New York: Doubleday, 1990).

21 *The Loyalty Effect*, Frederick F. Reichheld (Boston: Harvard Business School Press, 1996).

21 "Zero Defections: Quality Comes to Services," by Frederick F. Reichheld and W. Earl Sasser, Jr., *Harvard Business Review*, September-October, 1990.

21 *Raving Fans*, Kenneth Blanchard and Sheldon Bowles (New York: William Morrow and Company, 1993).

22 *The One-to-One Future: Building Relationships One Customer at a Time*, Don Peppers and Martha Rogers, (New York, Doubleday, 1993).

22 "The Four Faces of Mass Customization," James H. Gilmore and B. Joseph Pine II, *Harvard Business Review*, January-February, 1997.

22 *One Size Fits One*, Gary Heil, Tom Parker, and Deborah C. Stephens, (New York: John Wiley, 1997).

23 "Measuring Customer Satisfaction: Fact or Artifact," Robert A. Peterson (Austin: University of Texas Working Paper). Quoted in "What's Love Got To Do With It," Ron Zemke, *The Service Edge Newsletter*, January 1991, p. 8.

33 *The Ordeal of Change*, Eric Hoffer, (New York: Harper and Row, 1962), p. 79.

51 *Love and Will*, Rollo May (New York: Dell Publishing, 1969), p. 312.

56 "After the Sale Is Over...," Theodore Levitt, *Harvard Business Review*, September-October, 1983, pp. 88-94.

57 *Howards End*, Edward Morgan Forster (New York: Knopf Publishers, 1910).

72 *Knock Your Socks Off Service Recovery*, Ron Zemke and Chip R. Bell (New York, Amacom Books, 2000).

Bibliography

91 *Managing Knock Your Socks Off Service*, Chip R. Bell and Ron Zemke (New York, Amacom Books, 1992).

107 Lyrics from "It's Alright, Ma (I'm Only Bleeding)." Copyright © 1965 by Warner Bros. Music, renewed 1993 by Special Rider Music. All rights reserved. International copyright secured. Reprinted by permission.

118 Tuay, Duane C., "A Construct of Trust," Ph.D. dissertation, University of Texas, 1994

150 *High-Velocity Culture Change: A Handbook for Managers*, Price Pritchett and Ron Pound, (Dallas, Texas: Pritchett Publishing Company, 1993), p.22.

162 *A Room With A View*, Edward Morgan Forster (New York, Knopf Publishers, 1925), p. 115.

ABOUT THE AUTHOR

 Chip R. Bell is a senior partner with Performance Research Associates, Inc. and manages their Dallas, Texas office. PRA has offices in Dallas, Minneapolis, Ann Arbor and Orlando and consults with organizations on ways they can build long-term customer loyalty. A renowned keynote speaker, he has served as consultant or trainer to such major organizations as IBM, Cadillac, Microsoft, Motorola, Lucent Technologies, Marriott, State Farm, Merrill Lynch, Ritz-Carlton Hotels, Bayer, Eli Lilly, Royal Bank of Canada, First Union, Aurora Health, Harley-Davidson, and Victoria's Secret. Before starting a consulting firm in the late 1970s, he was Vice President and director of management and organization development for NCNB (now Bank of America). In the late 1960s he was an infantry unit commander with the 82nd Airborne Division in Vietnam. Bell holds graduate degrees from Vanderbilt University and the George Washington University.

He is the author or co-author of 14 books, including *Beep Beep: Competing in the Age of the Road Runner* (NY: Warner Books, 2000 with Oren Harari), *Knock Your Socks Off Service Recovery* (NY: AMACOM Books, 2000 with Ron Zemke), *Dance Lessons: Six Steps to Great Partnerships in Business and Life* (SF: Berrett-Koehler Publishers, 1998 with Heather Shea), *Managers*

as Mentors: Building Partnerships for Learning (SF: Berrett-Koehler Publishers, 1996), Customers as Partners: Building Relationships that Last (SF: Berrett-Koehler Publishers, 1994) and Managing Knock Your Socks Off Service (NY: AMACOM Books, 1989 with Ron Zemke). He has written over 200 articles in such professional journals as Management Review, Quality Digest, Training, Executive Excellence, Training and Development, Services Magazine, Advanced Management Journal, Supervisory Management and Journal of Management Development (UK). Additionally, he has hosted four major training films on service quality and leadership.

On a personal side, he has been married for over 35 years to Dr. Nancy Rainey Bell, a public school administrator and attorney. He has one son, Bilijack, a commercial real estate specialist in Atlanta, and a daughter-in-law, Lisa. Chip is an enthusiastic fisherman and enjoys boating, music, and entertaining.

Chip R. Bell
Performance Research Associates, Inc.
25 Highland Park #100
Dallas, TX 75205-2785
Phone: 214-522-5777
Fax: 214-691-7691
email: chip@beepbeep.com
www.socksoff.com

Executive Excellence
publications are perfect:

- *As personal or professional vitamin pills. Executive Excellence* is an enriching monthly supplement to an executive's current diet of management and leadership training. *Personal Excellence* enhances the on-going personal and professional development programs of people at any age and stage in life.

- *As in-house management or personal development newsletters.* The magazines can be customized and received under an organization's own cover sheet.

- *As thought pieces for focus groups and management meetings.* The magazines can be analyzed and applied to help with current organizational dilemmas.

- *As a public relations gesture.* The magazines can be sent to favored suppliers and customers or displayed in reception and reading areas.

- *As gifts. Executive Excellence* may be given to newly promoted managers or to a management segment of the company. *Personal Excellence* may be given to all employees as a benefit.

Custom Corporate Editions
Corporate editions of both magazines are available. The magazine may be wrapped with a "false cover" with messages and announcements from the company, printed with the company logo, enhanced with articles by prominent company officers, or a combination.

Custom Reprints
Order custom reprints of your favorite articles (or chapters in this book)—in black & white or color—for use in your corporate training and development programs and seminars.

Foreign Language Editions
Executive Excellence is available in Spanish, Korean, Japanese, and Turkish, editions. English-language editions for Australia, Ireland,and India are also available. *Personal Excellence* is available in Japanese and Turkish languages.

Executive Excellence Publishing has other publications in a variety of languages. For more information on other special editions, please call 1-800-304-9782.